PHalarope Books

The Local Wilderness

Observing Neighborhood
Nature through an
Artist's Eye

Cathy Johnson

PHalarope
Books

PRENTICE HALL PRESS · New York

Published by Prentice Hall Press
A Division of Simon & Schuster, Inc.
Gulf + Western Building
One Gulf + Western Plaza
New York, NY 10023

PRENTICE HALL PRESS is a trademark of Simon & Schuster, Inc.

Library of Congress Cataloging-in-Publication Data

Johnson, Cathy (Cathy A.)
The local wilderness.

(A PHalarope book)
Includes index.
1. Nature study. I. Title.
QH53.J64   1987   574   86-43109
ISBN 0-13-610171-2

Designed by: Helen L. Granger/Levavi & Levavi

Manufactured in the United States of America

10 9 8 7 6 5 4 3 2 1

First Edition

Acknowledgments

I would like to express special thanks to those who were so unfailingly helpful in researching this book: Patrice Dunn and Tom Hein of Martha Lafite Thompson Nature Sanctuary in Liberty, Missouri; Burt Wagen-knecht, professor of botany at William Jewell College, Liberty, Missouri; Charles Newlon, associate professor of biology, also at William Jewell; Fred Ostby at the National Severe Storms Forecast Center in Kansas City; Dan Henry, weatherman at WDAF-TV, Kansas City; William Bell and George Byers, professors of entomology at the University of Kansas; and H. Wilson, endangered species coordinator, and John E. Wylie, natural history officer at the Missouri Department of Conservation. If I have made mistakes I take full blame; they don't reflect on my helpers.

I'd also like to acknowledge the help and encouragement of Ann Zwinger, Charles W. Schwartz, and Clare Walker Leslie, fellow artists-naturalists. We don't work in a vacuum.

The women of the Excelsior Springs branch of the Midcontinent Library have been incredibly patient and helpful in researching this book. I owe them my heartfelt thanks.

Mary Kennan and Sarah Montague, my editors at Prentice Hall Press, have been endlessly patient, endlessly encouraging, endlessly helpful.

Last but never least, my dear husband, Harris, deserves thanks and praise—and a good steak dinner!—for helping me through anxieties, deadlines, proofreading, and the many small details that go into producing a book. He always understands.

Contents

Foreword

I have met Cathy Johnson only through her letters, her writing, and her sketches; yet I've known her for years. We've walked the same paths, observed the same animal signs, turned over the same rocks and set them carefully back, held our breath at the same mushroom spores. Reading what she, as a skilled naturalist, writes gives me a comfortable, exhilarating sense of reassurance.

What do naturalists do? They write letters to each other, and they look at the world about them. The letter writing between naturalists has been going on for centuries. Joseph Kastner described the communications of eighteenth-century European naturalists in *A Species of Eternity:*

> Naturalists who never laid eyes on each other became intimate friends by virtue of the long and faithful letters they wrote to each other, year in and year out, until death ended their exchanges.

The old-fashioned naturalist—for that is what we both are—has an affectionate curiosity about almost everything that proliferates in direct proportion to the time spent in observation. It is an open-ended experience, never stultifying, never boring; most of all never disappointing.

Cathy Johnson's way of looking is both visual and verbal, and each complements the other. Drawing what you see makes you see more to write about, and writing about what you see makes you see more to draw. The combination is more than the sum of the two parts. This guidebook to competent observation stresses how and where to look and how to put together what you see. Observation is, clearly, like practicing the piano: The more you do it, the better you get.

I have always been charmed by the idea that people think you are doing something magic when you sketch. For myself, I'm firmly convinced that the image is already in the paper and the quiet concentration of eye linked to moving hand simply brings it up from there.

I am even more firmly convinced that putting down a tree or a squirrel or a bird in lines is as easy, if not easier, as putting something down in words. It is more direct. It requires only focused observation and practice.

It is merely a different kind of description—nonverbal instead of verbal. Drawing is *not* difficult. Why people are so put off by it I do not know. The lyrical, observant sketches that Cathy Johnson does are highly skilled, but then she *practices*. The readers who follow quietly after her and look over her shoulder will find themselves doing the same.

Cathy Johnson is a wanderer. So am I, passionately committed to wandering—that desultory garnering of landscape from east to west and sometimes north to south, no particular place to get to at no particular time, following a meandering path whose only virtue is that it promises good things just around the next turning. It takes a long time for the Puritan work ethic mind to discover that one is most productive when the mind and the shoulders are at ease, that focusing outward in disciplined observation allows the mind the greatest inner opportunity to create and to play.

Cathy Johnson and I wander in different places, but we set our sights the same. She writes of the joys of a city park, a country road, or a hidden stream of the Midwest, I of the mountains, canyons, rivers, and deserts of the West. In writing about these places we are both saying the same thing: Take time to look, to observe. If you look you will become curious. If you become curious you will ask questions and with every answer, be given more questions. As you learn you garner a precious knowledge that belongs to you alone. With that knowledge you begin to care. If you care you will not destroy. This is, despite occasional rumors to the contrary, the best of all possible worlds.

Admittedly, this is a low-key approach—possibly too low-key given the swiftness of today's environmental change. But understanding, once reached, will not fade in an environmental fancy of the moment. If you want bombast, dire threats of disaster, and finger-shaking moralizing, you won't, thank heaven, find it here. You will find the order of nature; a sense of things working well and going right, something that does not happen all the time in the peopled world.

This is a book of peace and plenty, to read on a snowy afternoon by the fire or to stuff in your backpack when you walk an isolated mountain trail. This book has more sustenance than freeze-dried food, and the only calories are for the mind—to nourish, heal, and expand.

Cathy Johnson discovers good things ticking away in leaf veins, stems, trunks, and roots. She finds harmony worth attention in the snail's helix and the jack-in-the-pulpit's flute. She notices something worth listening to in the woodpecker's syncopated tattoo and the redtail's cry. She sees light worth describing through the transparent wing of a tiny fly. She watches events worth describing in a squirrel's gnawing and the coming of the spring.

This is a joyful book, full of the snippets, scraps, and corners that make up the natural world. This book is, in short, a field guide to serenity.

—ANN ZWINGER

Preface

This book is an expedition through "new" but familiar territory: a discovery of the myriad worlds of nature in our own backyards and gardens. You will discover how to find the exotic close to home, wildlife in your backyard, the secrets of nature in your neighborhood park—and in doing so, perhaps find a lifelong study. We take these places for granted, but they offer us endless possibilities: new sights and sounds; birds and animals we may never have noticed before; a sense of wonder and challenge and a new appreciation of our own special naturalist's "tools"—our eyes and ears and minds.

Many books intended for amateur naturalists are really field guides: compendiums of facts, the results of someone else's research. This book encourages you to write your own field guide, to keep a naturalist's field journal on your own backyard or local park.

Many books for amateur naturalists will tell you the best tools and equipment to buy—sometimes at great expense. This book, on the other hand, attempts to make the study of nature accessible to anyone, no matter of what age or financial bracket; a how-to without much to come between the naturalist and his or her experiences. It's simple, really. A pencil and a notebook are all you need.

You will learn to see and question as a child does, with a fresh outlook, a willingness to look with "new eyes." You'll discover resources to find the answers for yourself.

You'll learn how to set up and use a field journal, how to form a long-term learning relationship with a specific place, and how to create your own self-guided nature trail. You'll discover new ways to see and feel and experience the world at your doorstep.

Peace of mind is hard enough to find in our frenetic world. We've forgotten where to look. We tend to think we have to go far away, at great expense; perhaps find a guru or a key. This book will lead you to the accessible places with the tools you already have available to you.

We naturalists are lucky to be able to find peace in one place that has so much to offer: nature itself. Naturalists are among the most fortunate people in the world. Who else gets to retain a child's sense of wonder? Who else is allowed to sit and simply think, paddle feet in the water, and watch a tadpole develop tiny legs?

Asking ourselves questions always brings fresh new answers, and the answers lead to still more questions, new connections, and new conclusions. This book will help you get started. Your own curiosity will provide the impetus to keep you going, perhaps all your life long. I've never known a naturalist to grow old in mind—in body, perhaps, but never in that sense of wonder that hopes for new discoveries in the simplest places.

This book gives you facts, to be sure. Much research and help from the experts went into its writing. Much more important, it encourages you to dig out your *own* answers—and shows you the tools with which to do it.

Field journal page.

Introduction

We tend to think of a naturalist's field of study as being exotic, removed, remote, unique—the coast of Scotland, perhaps, Darwin's Galapagos Islands, Burroughs's High Sierras, or even the icy tundra of Greenland. Naturalists through the years have explored and recorded the birds, insects, mammals, and plants of such remote habitats: artists-naturalists such as John James Audubon, Louis Agassiz Fuertes, and Francis Lee Jaques have returned with their field studies and paintings to the edification—and pleasure—of scientists and laity alike.

Given that, we might feel that everything worth exploring has been explored, or that scientists (biologists, botanists, zoologists, geologists) are the only ones capable or qualified enough to do such work. Scientifically speaking, that may be so; however, *naturalist* is not so much a title or a profession as it is a vocation—a calling, to those who have roamed and rambled since childhood, bringing home tadpoles, sloshing about in Mom's chipped Mason jars, to watch them turn (shazam!) into frogs; raising owlets to adulthood, or watching over the cocoon of a cecropia moth until it came forth changed like Lazarus, and suddenly beautiful.

The world is a wondrous place—*all* of it, not just the Galapagos or the Sierras, but the ditch by the railroad tracks where I used to trap tadpoles, the red rock hills of the Ozarks, the waterfowl-rich floodplains of the muddy Mississippi River, the peaks of the Rockies near Gunnison, the gently rolling prairies of Kansas and Nebraska, the skinny strip of wild flowers at the edge of a city cemetery, and my own backyard. It is the wonder of discovering the unexpected close to home that makes the world so interesting.

My favorite area of study is in a small-town park not three blocks away.

My town is like many others of some age. Parkland was set aside early on, around the turn of the century. It's not a large park, as the crow flies, only three blocks across at its narrowest. It stretches out, snakelike, for sixty-five acres. The land follows the creek bed of the Fishing River as it winds through the old spa town where Harry Truman first heard he had lost the election to Dewey (untrue!). A slough, a tiny reflection of swamps everywhere, is hidden in the wooded area to the northeast, a fertile, wriggling, creeping breeding ground for half the frogs and most of the mosquitoes in Northern Missouri.

A steep bluff rises from the creek banks in one particularly rugged area—Clay Cliff, as it is dubbed by the boys who vie to climb to the top in a local rite of passage. The soil horizons of the area are well exposed there for the amateur geologist. Fossil rocks, blue-gray shale, golden-hued clay, and black topsoil form a gigantic layer cake that towers over the creek bed's boulders, a layer cake edible only to the worms and soil organisms that populate their habitat.

Herons of many types—great blues, little blues, greens, and black-crowned night herons—make this rugged area home. The great blues were seen throughout the park until a walking path rendered much of their area all too accessible to joggers and cyclists. The shiest of these big birds are now seen—and only rarely—in the upper reaches where no established path has gone.

On the hill, black turkey vultures have their summer home, high in the old-growth forest. Early mornings, from spring to fall, I see them move stiffly as the warm thermals begin to rise from the valley floor, giving those enormous midnight wings the lift they need. After their initial clumsiness, they are the most graceful of gliders: swooping, soaring, circling like lazy cyclones in their quest for breakfast.

A crow tree stands near the seep in the limestone rocks deep in the forest. The crows roost here, conversing companionably like the elderly people in the lobby of the retirement high rise. I approach quietly to listen to their gossip, so uncrowlike in its soft, varied inflections, and they tilt their heads for a better look at the interloper.

Wild turkeys stalk secretly through the woods, given away only by their wild "gobblegobblegobblegobble." The old tom leads his harem of hens now boldly across the road, a courtly escort to the plump damsels (a Sir Walter Raleigh of the forest). Our local congressional representative feeds them from her patio adjoining the edge of the parkland.

Even deer are seen here from time to time: a whitetail buck picked his way daintily down the steep trail on the north end last winter, oblivious to the houses just across the creek where my godchildren watched. Tracks are often visible in the mud at creekside, and I've found their soft summer scat not fifteen feet from the road.

My hope, with this book, is twofold: to share in word and drawing what I have seen and experienced, studied and loved, and to help you to see what is there for *you*, by suggesting ways to learn from your own wild places, no matter how small. Even a city backyard can contain a wild area where birds and butterflies and even opossums may come. Nearly all cities, towns, and villages have some land set aside for public use. A vacant lot may be starred with flowers ("weeds," perhaps, to the city fathers), their nectar an olfactory beacon for insects and butterflies of all kinds. Birds will come to eat the insects, and an occasional flash of a shy mammal's fur may be seen even in a downtown parking lot. Canada geese have been known to nest on skyscrapers. Railroad rights-of-way may be a wanderer's habitat for all sorts of wild flowers and herbs, some indigenous and some, like tramps, staying for a while beside the tracks, having ridden the rails from halfway across the country. A minuscule ecosystem pinched off between two interstates near downtown Kansas City is a wonder of varied habitats, from swamp-loving cattails to towering oaks and sycamores. A red-tailed hawk took up vigil there, telling me that there's much life to study even in this area of less-than-half a city block.

Every area of the country has its own timetable. Wild flowers that bloom outside Atlanta in late February and early March first open their pollen-dusted landing strips to winter-hungry bees here in late March and April. In Vermont these same flowers may hibernate in the slowly warming soil until May.

Each place has its own special wildlife, also on a timetable of its own. Robins that summer in my latitude and points north stop by in January for a brief visit at my sister's home in Nevada. Many species are migratory, passing through area after area, season by season. Others may stay year round or are indigenous to one special habitat or ecosystem.

I want to show you how to relate what I have experienced in one particular park (with a few occasional forays into other nearby natural areas and my own backyard safaris) to the natural lands you may have available, from a special corner of a large city park to that small island of wildness preserved between converging superhighways. From these tiny corners of the world may come great discoveries—and if not that, then inner peace and a lifelong relationship with nature. If even one person discovers the wonder of nature as close at hand as his or her own backyard, I will feel justified in writing.

I will show you how to take notes on what you find, how to know what you are looking at, how to ask yourself questions that will start you looking in the right directions for answers, and how to recapture the curiosity of a child. I will help you to locate the resources available to identify and understand the things you find in your own park areas. Libraries are wonderful sources for this information, as are local colleges, state and local parks and recreation departments, and your state conservation commission or division of fish and wildlife. The many organizational resources available to the amateur naturalist include the Audubon Society, the Sierra Club, the Nature Conservancy, and the National Wildlife Federation. All of these, from the biology professor at your local college to the people who put out national magazines devoted to the environment, are there to help you.

I will show you how to use field guides and how to find those that are most useful to *you*. I will give hints on how to write your own field guide, chart your own path, and direct your own study—and perhaps a few hints on sharing this adventure of discovery with spouse, children, and other friends.

Each place on earth has its insects, birds, animals, plants, fossils, and characteristic weather patterns. My small-town park is special to me for what I can learn, what I can experience, and for the peace it brings. My small-town park *is* a microcosm—a world in miniature—that represents all. Go outdoors and open your eyes. Look. *See.* Take notes: Write your own personal field guide. A lifetime would not be too long to spend. As Henry David Thoreau put it: "In wildness is the preservation of the world."

The woods in winter.

Finding Your Own Special Place

Each of us needs a place of his or her own, not necessarily by ownership, law, and deed but by response and identification; a place where we can go to be quiet, to be renewed, to be healed; a place that teaches us its secrets and hides us when, childlike, we need to "run away from home."

We may love the sea, the mountains, the deep and varied woods, or the wonderful openness of prairie, and we return to these places again and again to be refreshed. If the shore is a thousand miles from home or the mountains an eight-hour drive, we won't often find the refreshment we need. Many of us store these needs for quiet and space and the experience of firsthand learning for our vacation, but such times come all too seldom and are often overloaded with expectations. We must find a special place close to home that can fulfill these needs for us on a regular basis.

It's a matter of keeping an open mind as much as anything. Yes, we may love the sea; but nature surrounds us, even in a Midwestern city. We need to open our eyes and see what we have and what is available to us.

Stop your car for a moment, as you drive to or from work or hurry to the grocery store. Turn off the motor, roll down the window, and *listen.* Discover a small island of time between your activities. Inhale the scents that fill the air when exhaust fumes have dissipated. Take a moment to

1

just *be,* even if you are only three blocks from home. Notice what is going on all around you as you sit quietly. If you sit relatively still or do something unobtrusive like note taking or sketching, in ten minutes nature will be back to normal, ignoring you as if you were invisible. Try not to talk, move around, or smoke. In inverse ratio, you will find that you will have stilled and calmed as nature has become more active.

There are many little oases of natural beauty, even in cities and small towns. If you have thought of your local park only as a place to picnic with the family on the Fourth of July or as the location of summer softball or Frisbee contests, look again: There may be small (or large!) wild areas nearby. Some even have well-marked nature trails, excellent for the beginning naturalist as well as the old pro. A large city may have an arboretum, plunked down in the midst of busy traffic lanes—a mecca for urban wildlife; or consider the grounds of a large city museum or hotel. Your own backyard is alive with activity: Watch the seasons change; insects and birds move through their timeless life cycles; plants sprout, flower, seed, and die. Even a housebound naturalist can find a special place in the world outside a window or in small houseplants. Wherever you are, bits and pieces of nature will shine through, inviting study.

Accessibility is the first criteria for retreat. My own special place is only three blocks from my home, but I'd never really "stopped to smell the flowers" there until the year my husband was laid off. Time on our hands and not much money prompted us to explore close to home, and we discovered a place that has filled countless hours and many field journals with sketches, notes, and observations.

Sheathed
May Apple,
April 19

This May apple grows where a bulldozer was to strip off the understory and topsoil.

ESCAPE

Running away from home isn't only for children: We all need these times apart. Our accessible islands of natural history can make all the difference by offering us chances for escape.

Escape in this sense needn't have a negative connotation. We may escape *to* as well as *from*. And escape has an interesting side effect. We are fed, but we learn to feed as well. We learn the needs of the earth and can appreciate them. We can then help protect these islands of sanity as progress threatens. We can see or anticipate the needs of animals and birds of a specific area in times of ecological stress. We can join with others to preserve these small islands of escape for those who will come after us.

HABITAT

Varied habitats can be found in our special places, no matter how small. They are spotted throughout my park. The old-growth forest snugs up against the open grasslands on the hill. The edges where they meet, called transition zones, are always active. Animals and birds often feed on the growth at the fringes of the forest, where deep cover is always close by for a hasty retreat.

The creek provides a number of habitats. Swiftly flowing sections alternate with deep pools where muskrats and beavers build their lodges or

Bank swallows, crayfish, and insects make their homes in the clay banks of a creek.

A Sunning turtle - and
a Swimming one
The musk rat picks another bit of dinner, ashore this time.

The water is home to many aquatic and amphibious creatures.

dens up in the muddy banks. Bank swallows and crayfish make these banks into multispecies apartment dwellings. The crayfish are both predator and prey. They feed on the plentiful small fish and shellfish, and they dine like kings when the tadpoles are hatching. Later they themselves meet a similar fate: Raccoons feast on crustaceans in the hundreds.

Catfish, perch, bluegill, bass, and their fry live here, their streamlined bodies flashing in the current. The herons enjoy the varied feeding opportunities. An oxbow swamp was formed when the small river changed its course. Now these stagnant pools are home for lazy, sunning turtles and millions of hungry mosquitoes.

The savannalike park on top of Siloam Mountain provides food and lodging for a hundred squirrels and bluebirds.

Look for variations in habitat in your own special place. You'll be paid with a variety of wildlife-watching opportunities.

HISTORY: NATURAL AND SOCIAL

A study of the natural history of your special place can include a study of its human history as well. When was the land set aside (*if* it was) and by whom? Who might have lived here before, and what use would they have made of the land? Many of the wild flowers we see in our strip of parkland may have escaped cultivation, if the area once was populated. Check your field guides to see if a particular flower is indigenous or a transplant. (Many "weeds" that we assume are native to our area were brought deliberately from another country—even the common plantain

Broad-leaved plantain; a transplant from the Old World.

that grows everywhere in yards and gardens was known to the American Indians as white man's footprint because this medicinally useful herb was encouraged everywhere the settlers went.) The beautiful purple spikes of loosestrife now threaten to choke out native plants in many areas of the country, and last-ditch efforts are underway to preserve the vestiges of the Midwest's once-endless prairies. Gayfeather and big bluestem were once common in the tallgrass prairie of the plains states. Now they are often reintroduced.

Your study of botany may lead you to find out which plants may have been among the very first. In our park a stand of equisetum (or horsetail) grows near the creek. This prehistoric plant was known as the pot-scrubbing reed by the Indians; the silica in the stems make it an efficient cleanser when tied in tight bunches and trimmed like a brush. There are twenty-five species of these ancient plants, some clublike in appearance, others

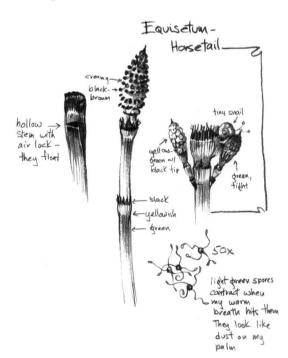

*Horsetail (*Equisetum*) study: My pocket microscope enlarged the amazingly lively spores to 50x. They squirmed and wriggled off my palm moments later.*

with rings of branches along the stem joints that give them the name of horsetail. These strangely beautiful plants are vascular, having roots, stems, and leaves with tubelike (vascular) connecting tissues. Remember your high-school botany: One set of these tubes, the phloem, transfers the manufactured food; the other set, or xylem, conducts water up from the roots. If you dissect a horsetail plant you will see the sections fit together with air locks at the upper end of each section, almost like a telescope—at 280 million years old, surely the oldest living prototype!

Wild onions also are prehistoric in form. These simple plants may have been among the first to be used by humans before the dawn of recorded history.

One of the best places to find relatively rare prairie plants may be along old railroad rights-of-way. These peripatetic plants (and many others) thrive along the older railways where use of herbicide is minimal or financially infeasible. They were carried there by the trains themselves, perhaps in the cracks in the floor of grain cars or in the cuffs of tramps, who were a common sight when I was young. Their seed remains viable, if kept dry, for some time. The plants we see now may have been the dormant progeny of plants that waved on the prairie from fifty to one hundred years ago. One of my favorite wild haunts is like a botanical garden by accident rather than design; the variety of plant life is astonishing.

CLOSER TO HOME

A nearby park, arboretum, or nature sanctuary may fulfill your need for escape and for the challenges of self-education as an amateur naturalist, but don't overlook opportunities even closer to home. Inky cap mushrooms may grow down the street. When they are young and before they begin to get black with the slimy substance that gives them their name, they are deliciously edible. A morel mushroom is more commonly found in the woods, of course, but one year we found one in our own fence row. A woman in a small Ozark town found an immense one growing in the crawl space under her house.

The common feeder birds are a delight to study—or simply to watch. Many birds go about their business totally unreceptive to our attempts to lure them. Chimney swifts chitter through the air on a summer's evening. Contrary to many people's experience with pigeons, ours treat us and our feeders with lordly disdain as they stalk back and forth on the ridges of the roof like magistrates.

When we see wildlife, we can be sure we are in its home range. Such a territory can be quite large, and we may be only on the outside edge. A quick check in your field guide will tell you how large a territory a particular creature will have, and if he or she patrols it often. Then you can tell how often you might see the creature if you are quiet, at the same time or place.

Aug. 6 – 8:30 am
cool, sunny, dew

stray downy

iridescent gray-blue

brown

BLUE JAY?

Turtles rise to the surface of the water over and over; Fishing River's answer to dolphins. They look like sliders.

swifts flying under the bridge where I stand

Squirrels have been eating the small green apples on the teacup tree. I would, too, if I could reach one – they are few, & high up

Psathyrella subspecies (L – almost black)

light tan cap, dark gills, white stem

Independent swifts ignore us with fine unconcern.

MAKING YOUR OWN SPECIAL PLACE

Everywhere there is much to see if you just stop and look. Even in the cracks in an urban sidewalk a chicory plant may bloom. Encouraging nature by making the backyard a hospitable sanctuary is rewarding. Nearly everyone can afford a backyard bird feeder and the seed to carry it through the winter, and seeds and grain may attract other animals as well.

But why stop there? The National Wildlife Federation or your state's department of natural resources or conservation commission can provide you with information on turning your backyard into a personal nature sanctuary. Many flowers and flowering herbs not only add immeasurably to the beauty of your backyard environment but also provide a welcome for hummingbirds, a variety of butterflies, and other nectar-feeding insects. A source of fresh water in the form of a frequently filled birdbath, a recirculating fountain, a fish pond, or even a dripping faucet will meet the requirements for moisture for insects as well as birds. You may see bees, mud daubers, or paper wasps at your birdbath along with splashing sparrows. You may also see mosquito larvae hanging like miniature shrimp in the water—to avoid *too* naturalistic a backyard you may want to dump this water often or float a thin skim of garlic oil on the top to discourage these bloodsucking pests.

A naturalist's garden is likely to be a far cry from what that same word conjures up for the serious gardener. We are simply too interested in plant or animal sports, plant "volunteers," and impromptu experiments for "good" gardening. A weed can be as interesting as a turnip plant and sometimes, if left to flourish, provides delightful surprises. Three gigantic mullein plants that threatened my small potato plot with extinction were nonetheless allowed a place because of their robust, towering beauty as well as their medicinal uses against a sore throat or a cold. Besides, I came to love the way a heavy morning dew bejewels each hair on their velvet leaves. These nearly ten-feet-tall sentinels now guard my garden plot, and as a reward for my tolerance I see a variety of insect life on the yellow blooms and beneath the pale velvet leaves. The best reward so far was the sight of a hairy woodpecker rappeling down the tallest stalk, supporting himself with his spiky tail feathers.

Below my pole feeder, an impromptu experiment in comparative plant growth is conducting itself while I watch. Last winter's sunflower seeds sprouted where they were tossed to the ground by messy feeders, some on the rich earth where they were protected from the mower by a corner of patio and walkway, others into an old tub planter that normally blooms with scented geraniums. One year I missed the geranium sale and the sunflowers sprouted there as well. This graphic show and tell is an unmistakable lesson about plant growth, available nutrients, adequate water, and the effects of overcrowding. The seeds in the tub, left unfed and unwatered except by nature's whim, are poor, spindly affairs. Few are setting seed at all, and further experiments of perhaps a more deliberate sort will tell me if they are viable next year. The sunflower on the small,

A female hairy woodpecker searches for lunch in the dried stalks of mullein in my garden.

protected triangle of ground, on the other hand, can search deep into the earth for moisture and nutrients and has competition only from a low-growing sedum. Its head is heavy with ripening seed: self-perpetuating bird feed!

Of course I am not proposing that you let your garden become an unsightly weed patch for the sake of nature study—the neighbors will complain and the city fathers frown on such eyesores. Consider, however, allowing a corner of your yard to "go wild." Protect it from the lawn mower. Provide wild flowers bought from a reputable nursery, not dug in the woods, and concentrate on those indigenous to your area for easy care. Make water available, and birds and butterflies will soon frequent this wild place as if it were their own private corner of the woods.

Creating a place from which to enjoy your sanctuary and observe the wildlife it attracts will complete this special area. My back-porch chair is only one possibility; a gazebo, a screened room, or a vine-covered arbor gives you pleasant cover from which to watch in camouflaged comfort. A child's tree house gives the amateur naturalist a bird's-eye view of the backyard. Even a hammock will disguise your two-legged humanity while giving you a delightful opportunity to observe at your ease. In winter a window opening onto the yard can provide an observatory.

Look for ways to enhance your home's attractiveness to wildlife. Even a city apartment can have window boxes, patio planters, bird feeders (some mount directly onto the window glass), or houseplants. On the days when you *can't* run away from home you may still have plenty to observe right in your own "backyard."

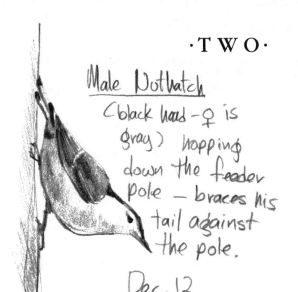

Male Nuthatch
(black head - ♀ is
gray) hopping
down the feeder
pole — braces his
tail against
the pole.

Dec. 12

Small birds are often among the first things that toddlers notice.

Learning How to See: On Becoming a Child Again

We come into this world with a burning curiosity about everything and anything with which we make contact. We want to learn, and quickly. Each small movement catches our eye, piques our curiosity: What's *that?* When we begin to speak, we drive our parents wild with questions time and again as we store all the information we can gather, asking over and over to see if we get a different answer this time or perhaps one we can better understand. We are curious about ourselves, our bodies: how we see, how we feel, how we think, how we *work*. We are curious about the world around us as well. Many babies first notice light outside or birds or small animals as they try out their new eyes.

Later as we learn the facts our curiosity abates. Knowledge becomes cut and dried. School has taught us, given us tests, and graded us on our knowledge. When we become teenagers, it is no longer "cool" to question so avidly, so naively; and adults become, sadly, much too busy, harried, hardened, and worldly.

Most of us, though, if we can stop and become our true selves, will admit that the curiosity is still there. The world is still magical, filled with mystery and wonder. Even those facts we know and those things we understand are subject to change. Some scientific theories that were accepted as fact as recently as fifty years ago seem as silly now as the notion of finding babies under cabbage leaves. Only by asking—and continuing to ask—do we begin to uncover mysteries.

SHARP EYES AND AN OPEN MIND

To acquire an open mind only a bit of retraining is necessary. We need to slow down, to look, and to *see* what we are looking at. It's easy to keep an open mind if we realize that we seldom know the final answers to anything at all. I am often amazed to see a bird, an animal, a flower, or a tree do something I thought was surely impossible. I have seen a lilac bloom in the fall and a blue violet in November. Amazement keeps me looking, seeking to find new answers. My own ignorance is staggering, a black hole in scope. It's what makes learning such a joy. Of course I'm ignorant (we all are)—what would be the point of continued study if I were not?

Developing sharp eyes is aided by note taking or sketching. As an artist, I often feel that I never really *see* something until I have attempted to get it down on paper. Not everyone is an artist, of course, but everyone can take notes. Everyone can see and describe a bird or animal, write down what it was doing, at what time and in what habitat, what sounds it made, and if it was alone, or with a mate or a group. Everyone can note the season, time of day, and place a particular flower bloomed, or which

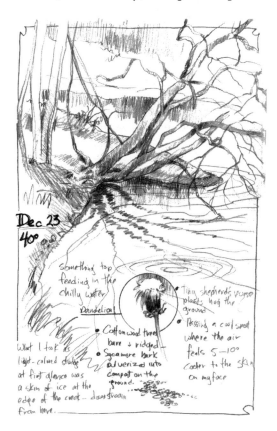

Who would have expected to find a dandelion ready to go to seed in December?

The varieties of oak leaves are astounding. Here we have serrate, lobed, cleft, and a sort of combination lobed-cleft, all from one family.

insects or birds seemed attracted to it. Learn the names of the parts of plants. Simply noting some of these names (such as pinnate, palmate, or lobed leaves) will help you to see the parts better and to find them more easily in your field guides.

A strange hieroglyphic in the snow says a bird has made this his launching pad.

Our eyes and minds become jaded by too many labels. At first, it is best simply to experience, to be quiet and look. *Then* note what you have seen. An open mind operates best where it's given room to work, not when it is pinched in by too many preconceived notions or facts learned by rote. Experience really is the best teacher. I quickly forget many facts I pick up in reading, but those same facts related to personal experience are mine forever.

If you are trying to familiarize yourself with a new species or learn more about one you thought you knew well, begin by asking yourself questions. Quite childlike ones will do—I am often sent off on one of my rambles by the most elementary what's *that?*. More elaborate questions can follow: What's it doing? Why is it here? Is it alone? Is it calling a mate? What does it eat (or, What is eating this)? Is it defending territory? When does it bloom? What are its seeds like? How do they disperse? How does it reproduce? What are its uses? What is its niche in history, in the ecological balance, in the food chain, or in art?

One question leads to many, and the answers can make a pretty complete self-taught education. Intelligent questions, and enough of them, will allow you to seek expert help if necessary as well. Don't try calling up a member of the Audubon Society and asking, What's that little brown bird I saw in the park? unless you have also answered for yourself questions about what the bird was doing, its approximate size or shape, where it nested, or if it was alone or in a flock. Your Audubon helper will be

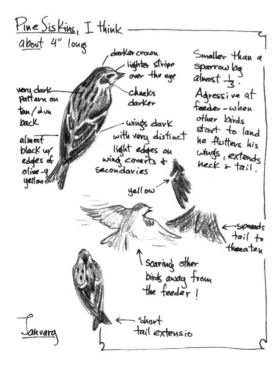

My rough sketches and marginal notes helped me identify Pine Siskins out of all the little brown birds in my field guide.

Field journal page. The creekside ecosystem is well represented here in equisetum, water willow, and thirsty robin. The small insect had an antic look; he resembles a mayfly, but not quite like the ones in my field guides.

nonplussed otherwise. There are simply too many little brown birds to choose from.

This fresh approach will allow you to make new connections. Last year's ruby-crowned kinglet turns out to be this year's goldfinch in winter dress! New connections are the basis for many self-taught conclusions, and they enable you to know where to look for answers from the experts. Anyone can think analytically, although the word *analyze* has developed negative connotations of late. One definition can be paraphrased as "to separate into the essential parts; to discover the essence of"; not a bad idea for an amateur naturalist. Answers to each question can describe or investigate an essential element of your subject such as growth pattern, habit, size, or color. In this way you can find the essence of any number of things in the park or the garden that were simply there before unnoticed, unnoted, un*seen*.

A NATURALIST'S TOOLS AND HOW TO USE THEM

Of course, the naturalist's best tools are those already mentioned—sharp eyes, curiosity, and an open mind. Once curiosity is aroused, we often find ourselves wishing for a new door or another path to find the answers to our growing list of questions. There are some common tools—binoculars, hand lenses, microscopes, telescopes, field guides, and journals—that can help.

BINOCULARS. Binoculars are often the first outdoor aid an amateur naturalist will purchase, and with good reason. Wild flowers, plants, and trees will all behave themselves and let you study them to your heart's content. Birds and animals, on the other hand, are notoriously shy of people. It is a real frustration to try to get near enough to that little brown bird even to ask yourself the proper questions—in summer they are only disembodied voices or flashing gray shadows in the trees. Even if you can get close, binoculars will help you to see in real detail.

Most useful binoculars are in the 7×35 to the 7×50 range. Seven refers to the magnification power, while the 35 or 50 refers to lens size in millimeters. Some binoculars are made especially to accommodate eyeglass wearers by compensating for the distance between the retina and eyeglass lens.

Good binoculars can be adjusted to fit your own particular vision by your closing first one eye and then the other while turning each individual eyepiece to the right focus. They will need no further adjusting except to fit the distance between your pupils; this is the purpose of the center-hinged design. Shop carefully and buy the best pair you can afford. Poor lenses halo the image and will give you a good case of eyestrain with extended use. Discount stores often carry very good brands at relatively low prices.

Prehistoric-seeming great blue heron, observed at Watkins Mill.

HAND LENS. This can be little more than a simple magnifying glass. Even a small boost will provide you with much more information than the naked eye is able to discern in the intricate workings of a flower's reproductive system or the anatomy of an insect. More professional hand lenses have two or more separate lenses that can be used alone or in combination to intensify magnification.

MICROSCOPE. If you really want to make visible the invisible, you will need a microscope. Unless you are planning a career in natural history, even a child's hobby model will prove sufficiently—and incredibly—revealing.

These tools are generally none too portable, so specimens are usually brought home to study. A drop of creek water is a teeming world in miniature when placed on a glass slide. (If you are the squeamish sort, don't put your drinking water under the lens.) A smear of petal or leaf is a stained-glass wonder of cells.

Microscopes have several lenses on a swiveling head for varying degrees of magnification. The hobby models often come as a kit. They will include, most probably, glass slides, dissecting tools, a stirring rod, test tubes, hand magnifiers, and an instruction booklet. Shop around. Many discount stores carry quite adequate models.

One of my favorite tools, a gift from my understanding husband, is a pocket microscope. It differs from a hand lens in that it has a battery and a light and magnifies up to $50 \times$. This is enough to study cellular structure of a leaf or a petal, grains of pollen, or insect eggs. A wonderful and portable tool, it is no larger than some pocket-sized flashlights. The only problem is remembering to buy batteries. It has an advantage over a regular microscope in that the light comes from above rather than through your subject, giving more accurate color information.

When you go into the field, take along some small jars, plastic sandwich bags, or test tubes to collect things to study later under your microscope. Be careful not to pick endangered plant species (your state will have a listing of these) or any plant that is the only one in a given area. A leaf or petal or two will be enough. Try a jar of creek mud at various seasons: It will amaze you to see the amount of activity in the mud of January, collected only by breaking the ice at creekside. Mushroom spores may be collected by placing the cap on one of your glass slides overnight and covering the whole thing to prevent its being disturbed. By morning you will have a perfect pattern of spores to study. Lichen, moss, and algae are fascinating at extreme magnification.

TELESCOPE. The type of telescope you buy depends on the use you plan for it. If you know beyond doubt that you will study only the stars, you'll need a celestial model. If you want to wildlife watch instead, a terrestrial model is for you. If you are like me a true generalist, however, you may

Field journal page. The barred owl here was really too far away to identify, except by call. His "portrait" was drawn at a later time from a more cooperative subject.

have to compromise somewhat and use a model designed for both purposes. As in most compromises you lose a bit in quality on both ends, but the versatility more than makes up for that loss. My scope will even take a camera mount for my amateur photography.

My telescope, which is by Jason Empire, has separate lenses for each use and has served my purposes well. Its 150×60 capabilities are versatile enough for the amateur naturalist if not for a professional wildlife photographer. A sturdy tripod is a must, though, both for prolonged viewing and for photography.

This is a rather unwieldy tool to take to the field, and unless I am going specifically to watch or draw birds and other wildlife I leave it at home. To protect an expensive piece of equipment like mine; many people carry their scopes to the field in their original cases and assemble them there. A more immediate solution is to fashion a sturdy carrying strap and sling the thing over your shoulder. I keep mine assembled and at the ready—otherwise, I'd never use it.

FIELD GUIDES AND REFERENCE BOOKS. As you ask more and more questions

Field journal page. The number and variety of birds on this November day presaged the migration from our area. The woods seemed strangely quiet a few weeks later.

that you cannot answer from personal observation, you will find that you are either spending many hours at the library or amassing a wide collection of field guides. Most amateur naturalists have their favorite guides, chosen for different kinds of virtues such as ease of identification, fine art or photography, or breadth of information. You may begin with a relatively narrow field of interest, such as bird watching or wild flowers, and then expand into other areas: weather, rocks, fossils, insects, or plants, for example.

When I decide to buy a new field guide I test it out first. Each book is organized differently and each one has different merits and deficiencies. I look up an animal, bird, or plant in the index. If I can find the test subject there, I turn to the indicated pages to see how much pertinent information is there. Some of the more useful guides have comparative subjects on the same page, plus maps of the area in which the plant or animal (or whatever) is found.

Portability and durability are important considerations for guides you plan to take into the field. A field guide too bulky or grand for the field is a reference book, no matter what it is called!

FIELD JOURNAL. Beyond my eyes and my curiosity, my own favorite tool is my field journal, a self-created reference. A simple spiral pad and a No. 2 pencil have provided naturalists over the years with a place to learn, dream, study, and conjecture. As an artist, I prefer unlined paper in a sturdy bound form, a study tool I could not do without. Memory is too chancy to trust for obscure facts or observations, especially when a lengthy amount of time has passed. Too much water under the bridge washes away a lot of information, but a few words jotted down on the spot, supplemented (sometimes, but not always) with sketches or drawings, has the power to bring it back alive for me. Years later I will recall the circumstances with almost brilliant clarity from only a few key words or phrases.

The questions your journal will be able to answer for you are those same questions with which we began this chapter: What's that? What's it doing? What does it eat? I try to write in my journal each day. I include the date, weather information, the place and any habitat notes, the time of day, and the temperature. Pertinent facts that seem pedestrian enough at the time may become meaningful later when I want to know when the last asters bloomed or when I might expect to find the first morel. (Weather conditions play a great part in natural occurrences like these. Droughts, floods, or extremes of heat and cold will affect blooming, migration, or hibernation dates somewhat, but the sense of continuity that notes provide is worth its weight in gold in these tricky and tempestuous times.) A sense of faith and of solidity is instilled when I see that, yes, last year as well as the year before the sun dogs fenced the winter sun with miniature rainbows at this time; that robins stayed in the park until late November this year as well as last; that spring comes and winter ends; that droughts pass and floods recede and nature restores her balance. Not only nature is healed in this restoration—I am healed as well. I've become a child again, in faith, in trust, and in curiosity.

THREE

Heron near the beaver dam

Anything out of the ordinary catches the eye, and should be investigated. The upright form of the heron, a stark contrast to the gentle horizontals and diagonals of the beaver's dam and pool, caught my eye, and I stopped to sketch him.

Eyes Only

SEE WHAT WE SHALL SEE

Telescopes and microscopes can afford tremendous acuity of vision, but these accouterments are also heavy, bulky, and unhandy, and sometimes the greatest pleasure and sense of freedom can be had by relying on our eyes alone. Like the bear that went over the mountain, we can use only our eyes—our amazing ocular devices—to see what we can see. It's more a matter of attention, really, than acuity of vision. If you are nearsighted and can't see clearly beyond six feet, there is still much to study in that short span. Whole microcosms open up at our feet if we pay attention.

Our eyes are marvelously suited for this kind of attention. One hundred twenty million photoreceptors called rods and cones line each eye, receiving light and translating the prismatic energy into electrical impulses that our brains then read much like a computer printout. They respond to low light, too; cones recede and rods advance as night falls so that we see less color but images are enhanced. Our vision will never rival the night vision of domestic felines. With 130 million photoreceptors they have us outnumbered. We can do without artificial light sources in the night world, though, and begin to notice a sharpened perception even in the flattened world of no color.

Train your eyes to discern movement, to differentiate between the dappled pattern of leaf and shadow and the spotted coat of a five-month-old fawn. Look for anomalies—ask yourself, What doesn't quite fit? One advantage of finding your own special place is that you begin to know it as well as the face of a friend. You know what to expect, what is the norm. Those spots of warm color suddenly seem too evenly spaced to be prematurely turning leaves: The light is shining through a doe's alert ears, turning them pink in the sunlight as she stares warily right back at us.

Look for these color differences. In the overall green of summer or the stark neutral palette of winter, color contrasts are most noticeable: the doe's pink ears or the startling blue of an indigo bunting against green; the flash of a cardinal or a rose-colored grosbeak against a bleak background. In full spring and in fall when color variations are everywhere, we need to look closer to know what we are seeing. Our familarity with a chosen area may make all the difference as to what we are able to see.

Sudden movements also help our eyes to differentiate wildlife from woods. A deer may freeze for many seconds and melt into the light and shade of the woods; if a deerfly buzzes her, however, she may twitch those big ears just as we would wave away the pesky insects. Foxes often make a sudden dash for cover; we may see a brush of tail disappear down a culvert.

In order to make the best use of our eyes, we need to practice our stalking skills. Shoes with soft, silent soles make getting within seeing distance easier, as does wearing a brimmed hat to disguise telltale eyes. Wild things are very sensitive to our eyes, and they know when they are being watched. If we are rude enough to stare we should at least disguise our poor manners.

Many animals that are frightened away by our threatening humanity might not be if we were to employ a blind, or *hide* as they are called in Europe. A car will act as a blind, and so will a tent or a simple shelter made of brush or reeds. If you are able to make a semipermanent blind near a mammal's den or a waterfowl feeding ground, you can keep your hands free and travel light to and from the site.

Try a portable, personal blind. A large poncho of soft material can make you unrecognizable if you sit near the base of a tree and spread the fabric, tentlike, around you. The brimmed hat completes your disguise. Camouflage fabric makes a fine poncho, and you can simply cut a hole for your head in a large square of material. I recommend soft fabric for its relative silence in the woods or in the wind; waterproof plastic may be practical in a drizzle, but it is noisy. During hunting season, bright orange is a better choice than camouflage. Most mammals are color blind anyway, and an excited or inexperienced hunter may mistake your crouching form for a deer. (Actually, another advantage of finding nature close to home is that there are very few hunters in parks and backyards!) The rest of the year I prefer the anonymity of invisibility as much as possible.

A certain openness to experience is a necessary ingredient to seeing. Be a generalist; if you go into the woods intent on looking for a particular wild flower or fossil you may miss the many things there are to see that are *not* that particular wild flower or fossil. A state of expectancy can heighten your visual awareness, but don't allow yourself to become totally fixed on a particular object. Tunnel vision may be useful when we must find a specific object, but a sensitized awareness will allow us to bring home visual treasures we never imagined.

LOOKING UNDER ROCKS (AND BARK, AND LEAVES, AND WATER)

Nature plays hide and seek with us. I see incredible things, broadcast freely, wherever I look, such as the fantastic shape of an antlered tree-hopper in the Southwest, or the mimic camouflage of a Polyphemous moth's starling "eyes." It's fun to open the *hidden* world to view as well.

By the creek or in the shallows, a rock may hide a fan-tailed crayfish or the more voracious rusty crayfish, *Orconectes rusticus,* which is now threatening the delicately balanced ecosystems in our Northern lakes. A spotted salamander may have set up housekeeping under your rock. Snails no bigger than a pinhead or tiny freshwater mussels look like a fairy's biology lesson.

Move carefully and gently, and lift these rocks *away* from you rather than toward you: It is possible to disturb the nest of a water snake. Most are harmless; a few, including water moccasins, are not.

Bark dwellers include insects of all kinds and their larvae. The loose bark of a dying elm hides the tracks of bark beetles and a nest of lined acrobatic ants. You may see a series of holes where a yellow-bellied sap-

antlered treehopper '85

An incredible "outer space" antlered treehopper in the Southwest.

A Catocala moth hiding under loose tree bark.

sucker has drilled to allow the sticky sap to come to the surface. The bird will return later to eat the insects attracted to this feast—a bird that plans ahead!

Moths may spend the daylight hours hidden beneath bark. A shy Catocala or underwing moth trembles in the light as I sketch it and then darts away as I look down. I see the wing tip beneath the undisturbed bark. These moths are seldom seen in daylight; they hide, their bright underwings folded out of sight.

The lined acrobatic ants have colonized the bark. My audacious inquiry into their private lives sends them scurrying to a safer place.

Smell this damp piece of bark. It has a rich forest smell, like mushrooms. Tiny white threads of mycelium are embroidered over the dark surface of the wood, acting as the "roots" of the more visible fungi outside the bark. When this mycelium is living in a symbiotic relationship with the roots of green seed plants, we call the arrangement *mycorrhizal symbiosis.* The fungus "roots" that break down decaying organic matter, such as the bark of dead or dying trees, are called *saprophytes.* Although mushrooms are sometimes considered parasites, that term really only applies when the host plant is damaged or dies from the relationship.

On the forest floor a white slime fungus looks as though someone spilled flour. Tiny scarlet cup mushrooms hide beneath rich leaf mold in winter and early spring and dot the path like drops of blood. I've found them as late as August.

The damp leaves have made a fertile nursery for baby plants. Seeds, fallen to the ground, are covered with these miniature blankets. In this protective environment they sprout undisturbed, and so a new generation of beeches, hickories, and red oaks begins life here. The leaves break down, decay, and become a part of the rich humus. If you are squeamish about bugs, you may wish to push aside the leaves with a stick; a great many small creeping things find a home here. The discarded white shells of snails as well as live snails and slugs may be hidden under rocks and decaying leaves.

Train your eyes to see through the clever camouflage of the wild creatures. Treehoppers masquerade as thorns, chameleons turn color to match their surroundings, moths startle with huge, owllike eyes or mimic tree bark perfectly in color and pattern.

When you want to explore underwater, it's not so hard as it might sound. You can construct a simple box with one glass side, sealing well with caulking. Push it into the water and you'll see a world normally hidden from us human observers; it's the same effect as a glass-bottomed boat. A scuba mask is a smaller, more personal solution.

Polarized sunglasses help us see through the glare on the water's surface without our ever getting a drop of water on ourselves. The shapes of fish and submerged snapping turtles, normally secure in their watery privacy, are suddenly as visible to us as if we had X-ray eyes. The glasses only allow light waves to vibrate in one particular direction, removing the distractions of glare and rendering the surface nearly transparent. Turn the glasses sideways and the vision disappears. Fishermen often use these glasses to help them find a likely hole.

Simply observing attentively can help remove distractions as well, of course. The small turtle here was visible after a moment or two of quiet contemplation during which I differentiated turtle-shaped shadows from rock-shaped shadows. It was exactly the same color as the rock it sat on.

BACK IN YOUR OWN BACKYARD

Don't take your own environment for granted. Although familiar, it's wonder waiting to be discovered. Dry rot and termites are sad things for the home owner to find and an apartment dweller often starts at the sight of an unwelcome midnight cockroach—but the amateur naturalist can enjoy a bit of study before the insurance adjuster or the exterminator arrives. After all, these life forms are far more ancient than our own; weren't we taught as children to respect our elders? They deserve a bit of respectful observation.

Patio bricks can hide whole civilizations. Lift one to peek underneath at the damp, fertile world. Take a magnifying glass, if you must, to the backyard—but most of all, train your eyes to see past the familiar. No

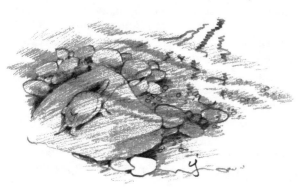

I saw only the turtle-shaped shadows as he rested underwater on a rock. His coloring blended perfectly.

matter how long you have lived there there is something new to see. Give it the same respect you would give an unfamiliar spot and it will open up to you like an old person with a thousand stories who's only been waiting for an interested listener.

Studies can be conducted here. Let your eyes be your guide. What is out of place? What is that flash through the trees? What kind of snake has the cat found under the cabbage? What is that wild flower volunteering by the woodpile? What will its seasons be (sprouting, budding, flowering, seed)? Your eyes alone can tell you its story. Just watch.

WHAT'S NEW? AND WHAT HAVE YOU MISSED?

As you look under rocks and bark, don't become so fixed and intent that you miss what is going on around or overhead. Other actors may come onto the scene and exit stage left without your ever seeing them. Be alert to sounds. Look up occasionally. As I sat on my favorite stone bench in the woods, a young pale green walking stick stalked out from under a cottonwood leaf and walked up my thigh. I brushed it gently away, for they have been known to sting humans. It played dead, lying on its back. While I waited for it to revive, I looked up to see a pair of mourning cloaks dancing overhead in the sunstruck leaves: a mating dance? A daddy longlegs crawled nearby. I was careful not to brush it; they exude an unpleasant scent to discourage predators.

If you see nothing under your rock, don't be discouraged. Look at the rock itself. It may contain fossils, remnants of preglacial life that might once have populated the very spot on which you stand. You hold millennia in your hand, prehistory in solid form. Perhaps the rock is of a particularly beautiful quartz, or it might be an ax head worked by our Indian predecessors.

Set a time when you "make your rounds"—not necessarily a rigid schedule, but a once-a-day, once-a-week kind of thing. This kind of loose regularity will help you keep a finger on what's new and what has changed

The beavers had taken down this eight-inch-diameter tree in only one night. It was a cottonwood; I wondered if they could have done the same with a tree with harder wood.

since you were there before. Trust me, even if it was only the day before, sharp eyes will detect changes. In my own park, overnight, the spotted jewelweed joined the pale jewelweed already in bloom by the creek; a brilliant explosion of orange as violent as a firecracker. Even a weekly checkup will help you keep tabs on the progress of a beaver's dam or the hatching of turtle eggs.

In winter these changes, invisible from even a short distance, will make you dizzy with their speed. Read the cottontail's story in the snow. Look closely to see when the snow fleas announce spring thaw. During a season of stillness and dormancy, things change fast outdoors in the cold months.

FOUR

Cottonwood leaf—
long, thin, flat
stem

*Long, flattened stems
let cottonwood leaves
bang together noisily.*

Using Our Other Senses

Our eyes are wonderful tools for observation and learning. Sometimes, however, we put too much emphasis on seeing, to the virtual exclusion of our other senses. Our wild counterparts in the woods, prairies, deserts, and swamps use all their senses in varying degrees, according to their sensitivity, need, or acuity. Bats locate their prey by echolocation, a process akin to sonar and the auditory equivalent of radar, but they are almost blind. Many animals (such as cats and hawks) not only see many times better than we do but also hear much more acutely (particularly deer, owls, and rabbits). A sense of smell is sometimes the difference between life and death in the wild, leading the seeker to food and water or warning of a predator lurking nearby. Turkey vultures are known to locate lunch by means of their acutely developed sense of smell as well as by sight; oddly, black vultures do not seem to have this peculiar talent.

Skin surfaces are incredibly sensitive to environmental factors. Beyond the obvious, heat and cold, skin can tell us of dryness or dampness, roughness or smoothness, still, windless air or the slightest breeze.

We've lost much of our primeval sensitivity. Disuse coupled with the distractions of modern life desensitizes us to the point that we live only half-conscious—if that!—of what is going on around us. This needn't be the case. A determined amateur naturalist can retrain senses, honing them to act again as invaluable learning tools. Of course we'll never have the night-seeing capabilities of a house cat or a sense of smell that rivals a bloodhound's, but we can sharpen our senses to the best of our ability.

HEARING AIDS

If our eyes seem to be wonderfully complicated machines, our ears are relatively simple. The outer ear funnels sound into the external canal, from which it proceeds to the eardrum, the hammer (malleus), the anvil (incus), and the stirrup (stapes), which are tiny bones that vibrate against each other. The vibrations cause sound waves to travel as messages to the auditory center of the brain, where they are separated and interpreted as sounds that make sense to us: words, music, bird songs, wind.

We don't need a mechanical aid to our hearing, of course, unless we have an actual medical condition. We *can* make use of simple aids to learn to hear—and to pay attention to what we hear.

First, be quiet. Shut off all distractions like radio, stereo, and television. Leave the house if necessary, but find yourself a quiet place. It's best, unless you have a very cooperative companion, to do this alone. Spouses, children, or other friends are wonderful for sharing nature with, but just now we want to be as close to silence as we can get, not only physical silence but inner silence as well. To focus on this one sense I often close my eyes or take off my glasses.

Sit comfortably or lie down if you can do so without falling asleep. If you are used to yoga, try a lotus position; if not, any comfortable position will do. (Often an artificially assumed position only serves to distract.)

Now listen. Be aware of everything you hear without judging it or naming it at first. Just let the sounds flow into your waiting ears. Now try to track these sounds mentally back to their source. What is that muffled noise? your breath? your heart? rain on the sidewalk outside? a hum of insects? Separate these sounds, let them form a kind of symphony in which you can distinctly hear each instrument.

If you are doing this outdoors, focus on one particular sound and actually track it to its source. Listen; true katydids actually say their name:

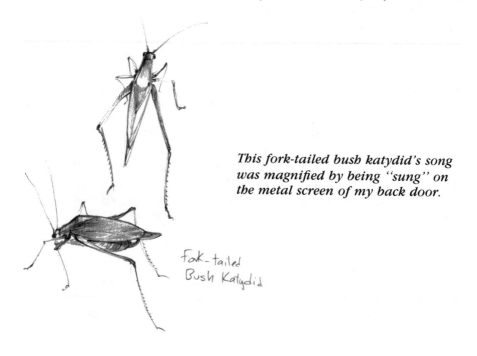

This fork-tailed bush katydid's song was magnified by being "sung" on the metal screen of my back door.

Fork-tailed
Bush Katydid

"katy-di-i-i-i-i-id." You may follow the sound to one of these long-legged green creatures looking a bit like the Martian in a 1950s space movie. An odd, jungle-sounding call may turn out to be that talented fellow with the big vocabulary, a blue jay.

Sit near a riffle in a stream—or in it, if you prefer. Find a place that is not so violent or swift as to make a constant roar but is a comfortable, bite-size rapids that speaks with many voices. Close your eyes and listen to the sounds of moving water.

As you sit and listen and begin to *hear,* the various instruments will separate themselves from the whole. A rock raised above the others lifts the water into a hollow curl; an oboelike sound, low and rich, results. A shallower riffle, like liquid lace, makes a rapid rustle like brushes on a snare drum. A miniature falls adds its own small voice.

You will be able to tell the depth, the speed, and the sort of bed (sandy, rocky, muddy) of your particular creek simply by the symphony it plays. Still waters run deep is more than an aphorism—it is a direct observation from nature. The noisy, laughing current of a rocky riffle is shallow and easily waded. Look here for the silver darts of feeding minnows. Hollow gurgling indicates the presence of larger rocks or other obstructions; crayfish, turtles, or even large fish may shelter here, ready to leap out to capture prey.

Many animals have large ears to help them capture sound waves and funnel them toward the ear canal. (Think of a kit fox, a rabbit, or a whitetail deer.) These big sonar disks swivel to catch the slightest sound. Take a lesson from the creatures and cup your hand behind your ear to increase its sound wave–capturing capabilities. You may have seen someone with a hearing disability do this; an old-fashioned ear trumpet carried the concept to an extreme. Satellite disks are, in effect, the same phenomena on a much larger, more technological scale.

A device such as your cupped hand can help you locate and translate sound in your park or your backyard. In the outdoors sounds seem sometimes to come from all directions at once; they may bounce off a nearby hill or echo deceptively from a cliff or through a gulch.

You may also take a page from the Indians' book. Put your ear to the ground, or against a tree. You may hear the gnawing of insects under the bark or the sounds of an animal in its den. You may even hear the peeps and squeals of a young beaver in its lodge. A doctor's stethoscope will let you hear the sap traveling through the veins of a tree if you are very still.

Sounds can be deceiving, but it's fun to listen for mimic sounds just the same. Every child knows you can hear the ocean in a seashell; have you listened since you were young? Make other connections as well. A sycamore's leaves make the sound of rain. The wind howls like a wolf. Certain birds make the sound of a drop of water falling from a great distance. Stretching your imagination will help you to notice, to hear, and to pay attention.

TAKING AN AIR BATH

Ask most people what our body's largest organ is, and if you don't give them time to think, nine out of ten will say the heart, the liver, or the stomach. Actually our largest organ, averaging 12 percent of the weight of the body, is our skin. Sensitive to heat, cold, and touch, this organ protects us, helps us control our personal climate by cooling us when we're overheated, and lets us experience our tactile environment.

A sense of touch is invaluable. We learn about ourselves and our surrounding from our earliest experience by touch. Sensing warmth, dryness, safety, and mother may all be a function of this one sensory experience. Our sensitive skin makes discovering our world a highly personal adventure; our most visible frontier goes with us everywhere. Our journey needn't stop at childhood. Looks can be deceiving. Many objects in nature look as if they might feel prickly when instead they are velvety. You might expect a pool to be cold when instead it is quite warm from an underground spring. The varieties of tree bark have to be felt to be realized.

Explore your sense of touch. Touch your fingertips together, and then run the fingers of one hand down into the opposite palm. You may find it much more responsive to touch than your fingertips. Your cheek, the inside of your elbow, and your lips are all touch sensitive. Try brushing your lips against a leaf to see what it really feels like. (Of course you might be accused of druidic leanings. That's all right; try it anyway.)

With sunbaths getting their share of adverse publicity these days, and with water baths being somewhat old hat, why not try an air bath instead? Taking an air bath is a delightful way to learn about your tactile environment. A nature sanctuary leaves the grass next to the mowed paths long, soft, and inviting. The grass bends back on itself to make a dry springy cushion that insulates against damp and cold.

At ground level, lying on my back in the dry silvery grass, the air is much warmer than it is when I'm walking. The skin of the eyelids, much thinner and more delicate than that of hands and feet, lets the light of the sun shine through in changing, moving scarlet patterns. The purpose is to notice the differences in environment on whatever skin surfaces we are able to expose depending on season and privacy.

Try going out at different times of day. See what it is like to experience nature directly, as animals do. Go out at night, in the sun, in the shade, in a damp mist, in a hard rain, or even, briefly, in winter's chill. You will understand much more fully what it is to be in contact with the earth and the air.

SMELL: OUR OVERLOOKED SENSE

We think of animals as having a much more acute sense of smell than we do. Perhaps this is so, but we ourselves have incredible capabilities that usually go unrecognized. We are capable of discerning a long series of scents coming into contact with the scent receptor at the top of our nasal passages at the astounding rate of three per second; our response time to each is only a few milliseconds. Not too much is known about the way the sense of smell actually functions. The *why* if not the *what* remains something of a mystery. Only forty-one molecules of a given substance are enough to trigger the olfactory receptor. Airborne particles are everywhere, teasing, bombarding, and whispering to our sense of smell.

Why are we not aware of the parade of scents as they enter our body? Colds, allergies, and sinus conditions desensitize the odor receptor, as does sensory overload and our tendency to mask natural odors with heavy artificial deodorants and room fresheners. It's too bad we resort so quickly to artificial scents that we very nearly lose our ability to experience natural ones. Just plain lack of attention plays a part as well. Since we don't need to be aware of the scent of predator or prey, we simply have learned to ignore it.

Think of the smell of newly mown hay (or freshly cut grass, if your experience is more urban), the first raindrops in the powdery dust after a long drought, the brimstone smell of lightning, the damp earth scent of a creek bank, the rich humus of a forest, or the smoky tealike aroma of autumn leaves. These smells have an almost magical ability to transport us to another time and place. The emotional leap from first scent to a sense of déjà vu or nostalgia through the mysterious corridors of memory and experience is faster than we can begin to measure.

As amateur naturalists we can retrain the sense of smell to an amazing degree, simply by making ourselves aware. To the questions we asked ourselves in chapter two, add this one: What does it smell like? Almost everything in the natural world is scented in some way, although not always pleasantly. The same earth that produces sweet violets may also sprout skunk cabbage or stinkhorn, those fetid-scented fungi that most

Stinkhorn in the yard!

The fetid, olive green cap of this stinkhorn was eventually carried away by flies!

Fruit-scented, edible, golden chanterelles.

often—fortunately—grow only in deep woods. We often think to "stop to smell the flowers," but try sniffing at tree bark, a stone, or a mushroom (chanterelles are delightfully fruity, with a delicate apricot scent). Smell the spicy scent of the dead stalks of bergamot; bruise the bark of sassafras; and sniff a skunk cabbage, a stinkhorn, or a piece of dried scat! It won't hurt you, and you'll be more aware of your environment.

THE AMPHIBIOUS NATURALIST

Our natural element is air, not to fly in, of course, but to breathe and to move through. Our skin responds to the movement of air. Every day we move through its caressing envelope.

There is a theory that we arose from the sea, squiggling from the mud and water until we stood upright on the land, lost our gills, and couldn't go back without them. Whether this is true or not, water is certainly our second home. Each of us has lived in the womb, swimming like a little tadpole in the rich soup of nutrients. This saline liquid is not so very far from the sea.

Water is everywhere in varying degrees. Our bodies are largely made up of water. We require water to continue life. The old saw that we can live three minutes without air, three days without water, and three weeks without food may be a old wives' tale (near drownings in frigid temperatures have resulted in a number of amazing cases where the victim was revived seemingly unharmed after long periods of time) but it points to the essential nature of this liquid.

As amateur naturalists we can rediscover the effects of water in many ways. Swimming, floating, bathing, and showering are all familiar enough to most of us. Try exploring water resources as you would a forest path or a prairie meadow. Jump in; the water's fine. See what happens: how it feels, how it sounds, how you feel at once light and buoyant as you float and heavy and dreamlike if you try to walk through the shallows.

Lie down in a creek or a pond. Let the water cover you. Lie in a riffle if you like, and listen to the sound of water rushing over the small pebbles and past your ears. Lie near the shore of a lake and listen to the lap of waves in a much more immediate way than you normally do on land. See what it feels like to be a frog.

In winter, put your hand through a lacy skirt of ice at a puddle's edge. See what the crystals feel like. Examine them closely to see how they were formed. Explore the patterns. As with snowflakes, you will never see just this design again.

Walk on the water? You and I can only do this in the dead of winter when the ice is thick. If you know the water is shallow and you are close enough to home not to risk frostbite or hypothermia (overchilling), experience how it feels when the ice is just forming and is a creaking slow-motion trampoline of glittering blue white.

Listen to the ice. You can hear it melting as well as forming. You can deduce the temperature from its sounds, the clicks, creaks, and whispers. Listen to the ice when you walk out on it. If you listen closely it will tell you how deep it is, how thick—and when to get off in a hurry!

ON THE HOME FRONT

Our sensory explorations needn't take us far from home. In inclement weather we may prefer to take our safaris—day or night—in small doses. The garden is always available, as are the yard, the back stoop, the balcony, or the fire escape. Listen to the sounds of chimney swifts chittering overhead before they disappear, by ones and twos, into their sooty home for the night. Listen for the squeak of bats near a streetlight. Their rapid squeaks for echolocation are inaudible to the human ear, but the small noises they make when startled or mating are easily heard if we listen.

Step out your door first thing in the morning. If you are an early riser you may feel the dawn wind, pushed ahead of the rising sun. The earth smells fresh. In winter the freshness crackles in the tiny hairs in your nose. Night birds are just ending their songs, and the first sleepy robins may sound their single notes. Follow an unusual scent in your garden to a new wild flower or weed. Experience your backyard by touch as well as by sight and scent. The textures of our immediate environment are as interesting as those of woods or creek. Discover what it is like to walk barefoot in the snow or over frost-stiffened grass (it almost burns). If you are close to home you will be soon warmed and none the worse for wear.

BLIND GUIDE

If you have a companion you trust, someone who also knows and cares about the small wildernesses close to home, act as blind guides to each other to enhance your sensitivity to what is going on around you.

Have your friend take your hand and guide you down a woods path, by a creek, or across a savanna silently. Don't talk unless absolutely necessary (a drop-off of more than six inches or a copperhead in the path is reason enough). Keep your eyes closed while your guide leads you along; use all your senses except sight. Feel the texture of tree bark, and try to identify the tree or simply identify *with* it. If you are in the woods on a windy day, feel the trunk sway even at ground level. You will be able to tell when you are in deep woods where the trees have grown tall and slender in their competition for the light.

See if you can tell if you are near a cottonwood just by the sound, or perhaps by the light touch of "cotton" on your face. Ask your companion to let you smell leaves or mushrooms along the way, and stop for bird song. Imagine what it would be like to be a night creature or a blind cave dweller. Do you see how much you might have missed by relying too heavily on one sense?

Now do the same for your partner. Take him or her, eyes shut, to a special place. You will develop mutual trust as well as sharing a special sensitivity.

If you have no one to go with you, be your own blind guide. For safety's sake you may wish to sit quietly in the woods and listen, touch, and smell. (Be sure before you close your eyes that you aren't near any poisonous plants.)

Try it—carefully. You will awaken capabilities long dormant.

FIVE

Field journal page. Earth and its life forms—past and present—caught my eye. In November there are fewer distractions.

Going to Earth

We take the earth for granted. If we think of it at all, we think of earth in some cosmic, global terms: *the* Earth; terra firma; our planet. We may be concerned about problems of feedlot runoff, industrial pollution, or underground testing of nuclear devices still carried on at alarming rates, but seldom do we consider the actual earth beneath our feet.

Those of us who depend on earth for our immediate living (of course we all do ultimately), such as farmers, orchardists, organic gardeners, herbalists—and naturalists, have a more intimate understanding of the soil and its workings, its inhabitants, its makeup, and its needs.

Pollution is not the only problem our earth is heir to—the erosion of topsoil is just as dangerous and damaging. It is estimated that eleven tons of soil are lost each year from the average acre of earth in the Midwest where I live. Worst-case acres may lose as much as one hundred tons where poor farming practices and old or poor soil with little organic matter team up with wind and water to scour the topsoil down to bedrock. Chemical fertilizers burn up organic matter, destroying tilth and reducing it to little more than something to hold our plants upright. In third-world countries, slash-and-burn agriculture exposes thousands of acres to erosion and loss.

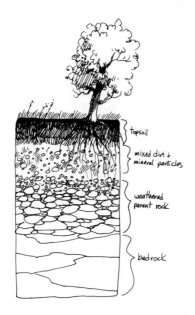

topsoil

mixed dirt + mineral particles

weathered parent rock

bedrock

Typical soil horizons.

SOIL HORIZONS

Like a giant layer cake, soil is striated, marked by the changes in climate and population it has undergone through the ages. A geologist can tell history in a glance by looking at a bare hillside.

Nine basic soil groups plus miscellaneous categories make up this layer cake. A map of the United States with its varied soil groups looks like a giant crazy quilt, with alfisols (fairly fertile and middle-aged) sandwiched between histosols (rich in organic peat and very young) and mollisols (young to middle-aged, rich and dark brown). Each soil group has a different horizon. Mollisols go deep, with the fertile soil that lured generations of farmers to the Midwest. Middle-aged alfisols are quite striated, and ultisols have very distinct horizons with their thin, poor topsoil spread over yellow or red clay like peanut butter on a cracker.

Research your own area to find what sort of soil it has and what might have formed it. A rich organic layer of topsoil might have been the remains of a swamp. Old, poor, shallow soil might have been raked and dotted with a million stones by a retreating glacier. You may have soil as thin as a taco shell, with a layer of rocks immediately under it.

Dig a hole, if you will, to see for yourself what sort of soil is there, or if you can discern its layers. In some parts of the country you would very nearly hit China before you got below that rich black loam, but more commonly you will soon hit a clay subsoil or a layer of fine bits of mineral pieces mixed with soil. Weathered rock is the mother of this layer and may be found just below it. Underneath it all is immutable bedrock, the foundation of our earth.

FOSSILS

Hidden in these layers of stone, decorating rocks like raisins folded in a cookie, fossils are the prehistoric remains of plants and animals perhaps a half billion years old. We read the passing of the eons in their changing shapes and speculate about evolution by slow stages or rapid, adaptive leaps.

We marvel at the forms, virtually unchanged by time, of horseshoe crabs, cockroaches, and ginkgo trees. Equisetum today is much like equisetum that knew the earthshaking stride of tyrannosaurs.

Most fossilized remains are of plants or animals that had hard parts such as bones, wood, or shells that were buried quickly and anaerobically, sealed away from air, and not subjected to normal decay. Leaf shapes may be preserved where leaves left their film of carbon between thinly pressed layers of shale. An entire animal carcass may be found frozen in a glacier. An insect may be saved in amber, which is the solidified sticky resin of prehistoric trees. I have such a specimen. Even the hairy legs and delicate, veined wings of this tiny, mosquitolike creature are preserved intact, visible under my hand lens. Normally, though, we find only the hard exoskeleton, bones, teeth, or petrified wood.

Some fossils are casts. No part of the animal actually remains, but there is an impression, such as a stone footprint in what was once soft mud.

The greatest percentage of fossils are found in sedimentary rocks, which were once the mud, clay, or sand of prehistoric lakes, caves, or streams. Life forms were impressed into the soft earth or sank from their own weight. When the earth itself turned to stone they became one with it, as if sculpted in place by time.

Look in limestone or shale deposits for small shells, crustaceans, ferns, or fish. Desert deposits may be found in sandstone. Petrified dinosaur dung (coprolite) tells us of the long-dead creatures' eating habits. You may even find solidified mud cracks.

Look for tiny, round beads of stone either embedded in rock or loose on a pebbly beach. These are crinoid stem segments, which were often

Prehistoric sun and moisture resulted in this fossilized mud crack.

fossilized
mudcracks

used by the Indians as ornaments. Hold one in your hand; feel the round-
ness, run your fingernail over the segments. This was once a living creature, a sea lily (so called because of its flowery form). It lived beneath the
inland sea that covered this land—lived, hunted, ate, grew, died, and became stone. How does it feel to hold prehistoric life?

Look between layers of shale by a creek. Ferns have left their carbon
images there like a photographer's negative to become eternity in tangible
form.

WHO LIVES THERE, ANYWAY?

INSECTS AND WORMS. Soil is not simply a home for tree roots and mycelium, a repository for earth history, and a final resting place for the remains of leaves, mammals, and fallen birds. The earth itself teems with
life that is a kind of subterranean civilization of activity.

Earthworms burrow through the soil, digesting and enriching it with
their castings. Their tunnels aerate the earth and allow rainwater to per-
colate deep into the ground where it is available to the plants' root systems. In particularly hospitable places with plenty of organic matter for
nourishment and sufficient moisture, there may be as many as three million worms in a single acre. In their endless search for food, worms move
tons of soil each year.

These somewhat slimy denizens of the earth under our feet are interesting genetically as well. The individuals have both male and female sex
organs, but they still must mate with each other since they cannot fertilize
themselves. This insures a strong and healthy future supply of wigglers.

Go out in your garden, early in the morning after a rain. I was amazed
to see, glistening in the early morning light, pair after pair of matting
worms, their tails still firmly stuck in their respective burrows as they
extended themselves as far as necessary to find a mate. It looked like a
garden full of stretched-out pink rubber bands.

April 2...
the garden is covered
with earthworms
pairing. They don't com-
pletely leave their burrows
(can't find their way back), they
just stre-e-e-etch to touch and
mate. There are four or five pairs
in various degrees of extension early
this morning (By 7:30 they were
all done.)

Mating earthworms.

A heavy rain will bring hundreds of worms out of their flooded burrows. Watch them as they move their segmented bodies. Each tiny section is fitted with four pairs of backward-facing hairs, or setae, that help anchor the segment in its new position as the worm moves forward in sinuous waves. As a method of locomotion this looks a bit tedious, but it is efficient. Try to pull an unwilling worm from its burrow and you will find surprising strength in those gripping setae. Watch closely—one may close its burrow by pulling a leaf into the entrance hole.

Grubs and larvae of many kinds populate the soil. Tomato hornworms spend part of their life cycle as fat cigar shapes below your dirt. Cutworm larvae are greasy-looking white grubs you will find when you cultivate, especially in spring. You may strike up a firsthand acquaintance with a number of these creatures if you dig a shovelful of earth from your backyard. Keep it in a terrarium with a screen lid until the fat, wormlike grubs pupate or hatch. Many kinds of moths may fill your glass enclosure eventually with the fluttering of wings. An experiment like this will allow you to know which creatures in their larval form may come to lunch on your garden.

Centipedes and millipedes are wormlike creatures that are also segmented. Instead of pairs of bristles these creatures can have from thirty (centipedes) to two hundred (millipedes) legs. Despite their wormlike appearance, both of these creatures are arthropods and earthbound relatives of the lobster.

Centipedes are speedy, carnivorous, and equipped with a powerful weapon in the form of prussic acid, which makes them poisonous to each other if forced into close concentrations as well as to their prey. They emerge at night to hunt worms and other hapless creatures. Some (*Geophilus electricus*) are even luminous and glow in the dark—an eerie prospect!

Millipedes are slow-moving, harmless herbivores. Like earthworms, they are busy with turning leaf litter and other organic matter into rich compost. Some species can roll up in a ball like their cousins, the wood lice (childhood's "roly-poly bug" or pill bug).

Millipede

Herbivorous millipede, dark brown and glossy, found under a rock.

This wood louse or "roly-poly bug" (also known as a pill bug for his ability to roll himself into a tight round ball as protection against predators) goes about his work of breaking down soil in my compost heap. They may also be found in rotting wood or even in your basement or bathroom. They have been blamed for destroying wood in houses, but unfairly; if the wood is sound and dry the pill bug has no interest in it.

Wood lice, in fact, are probably the first bugs children approach without fear and with a budding naturalist's interest. These harmless gray bugs are almost comical when they pull their armored bodies into a tight ball. This is a very effective defensive gambit, protecting their soft underparts from predators. They seem to come in all sizes if not all shapes.

You may find a convention of ladybugs (or ladybird beetles) under a layer of rotting leaves. These familiar round, buttonlike beetles don't actually live underground. You will often find them helpfully feeding on the aphids on your garden plants. They simply overwinter in large swarms underground or under an insulating layer of leaves.

Beetles, slugs, crickets, spiders, ants, and termites share space underfoot, as do fat furry bumblebees. Although some bumblebees may nest in the eaves of your house (or in a well as I found when trying to help a friend install a new pump), most bumblebees make their colonies underground, perhaps in an abandoned rodent's den. When a bumblebee suddenly appears virtually underfoot, you might have inadvertently discovered the entrance to its underground home.

You may see bumblebees earlier on cool mornings than the smaller honeybees. Thick insulating hairs and fat bodies act like down coats, letting the bumblebees forage without competition during the hours when other bees are still flexing their sluggish wings.

Ladybird or ladybug beetle, a highly useful little insect. When cottony-cushion scale threatened the California orange-growing industry, an Australian strain of these small beetles was imported. They were credited with saving the orange groves. Many organic gardeners buy ladybugs for use in their own gardens to fight aphids and other pests.

Many magical-seeming bugs populate your backyard plots. Look for mole crickets hiding in the soil. With their strong forelegs they dig through the earth just as efficiently as their mammalian namesakes. Trap-door spiders, dung beetles, and other specially adapted creatures help make backyard study a fascinating adventure.

SOIL MICROORGANISMS. Even in a single handful of dirt, life goes on at an astounding rate. Nematode worms actually swim through the soil in suspended water. A worm might be captured and digested by a specially adapted fungus present in the soil and leaf mold. The fungus lassoes nematodes and holds them in a death grip until it extracts their nutrients.

Mites, bacteria, springtails, and other microscopic life forms are also as present underfoot as they are in the smallest drop of water. That sweet smell of freshly turned earth in your garden or field is caused by lacy actinomycetes in the soil. Use your hand lens or microscope to discover what is living in your handful of dirt. With as much activity as is present in the soil, it's a wonder we can keep our footing at all on the moving earth.

MAMMAL DENS. Invertebrates and microorganisms are not the only denizens in the soil blanket. Mammals dig simple or complex homes or take over the burrow of another. In our area, woodchucks, gophers, badgers, weasels, shrews, ground squirrels, moles, chipmunks, muskrats, voles, mice, a transient opossum, or even foxes or coyotes in the breeding season may be found underground. A den may range from the large excavation of a coyote to the three-fourths-inch hole dug by a least shrew. Many "snake holes" are in fact the den holes of these small burrowing animals. (Most snakes don't actually dig holes.)

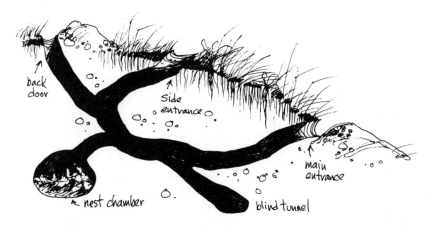

A prototype mammal's den; many different species use a similar system of tunnels and chambers.

A family of foxes.

Look for signs of digging or other activity along old railroad rights-of-way or on hillsides, especially where cover is available nearby. Freshly turned earth may give away the location of an entrance, but be warned: Most denning mammals dig a number of escape routes. I waited patiently for an hour near a fox's den on our old farm only to find the whole fox family calmly observing me when I finally gave up and turned to go back to the house.

UNDER THE FLAGSTONES, AROUND THE BACK

Depending on time of year, degree of moisture, and type of soil, you may find all sorts of life in the soil under patio or rock-garden stones. Pill bugs and earthworms have built their mazes. Tiny white mites scurry for cover. Lined acrobatic ants gather up their eggs and run when I lift their flagstone roof. Millipedes slither away on their wavelike feet. A flat black beetle is startled by my invasion of its homestead.

The roots of many small plants and weeds invade the sandy soil between my flagstones and reach beneath to form a lacy network. What was only sterile sand a few short years ago has become a rich mix of soil and organic matter, cast-off exoskeletons, roots, and the burrows of earthworms. Earth is in a constant state of flux—birth, change, death, and decay.

THE COMPOST HEAP

The compost heap, humus in the making, is earthworks on purpose. Here, using what we know of soil formation, we can encourage the raw materials of leaves, grass clippings, weeds, garbage, and moisture, with just a soupçon of earth for a starter, to become new earth. Kept moist, this salad will turn to rich humus—soil—in a matter of months. It is a time-lapse demonstration of nature at work. Earthworms, pill bugs, and millipedes infiltrate the heap from the bottom, looking for free food and enriching and breaking down the baby soil. Rain seeps through from the top of the barrel, keeping everything moist and working (a dried-out compost heap simply sits there). The microorganisms present in the occasional shovelful of earth and the boost of nitrogen in the form of manure also work together to make new earth. In the woods, under leaf mold, the same thing is happening without our help. Earth replenishes itself—often, tragically, not so rapidly as we use it up. If conditions are right, fertility returns—if we let it. If we help it along, as in my old compost heap, we're ahead of the game.

SIX

This field journal page shows the date, temperature, time, weather conditions, plus written and drawn notes of what I observed on one particular winter day.

Writing Your Own Field Guide: A Journal of a Naturalist's Travels

"WORDS AND MUSIC"

I need to keep a field journal—the words *and* music, as Ann Zwinger says, because it keeps alive the delight in discovery. I need to keep my own notes, my own sketches, and my own observations along with the digging out of facts from someone else's field guide. I've become intimate with the things I've drawn. They're friends and they're mine, in the sense that I can recall them later, often without referring directly to that day's entry in the journal. The intimacy and concentration of direct observation over the period of time it takes for on-the-spot notes and a few quick sketches seem to fix the subjects in my mind. I may misfile the name in the often-chaotic clutter of my inner computer, but I'll never forget the face.

Some things need to be drawn and redrawn, over and over, to understand them, to get inside them, and to touch their spirit. A certain odd joining of leaf to stem needs to be explored closely, with my pencil point crawling antlike over its contours, time and time again—of course, that crazy sunflowerlike plant with the leaves that seem to form a bowl around the stem: cup plant! How could I forget? The name comes without my bidding it, last year's minnow caught in the seine.

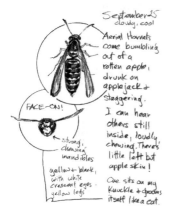

September 25
cloudy, cool

Aerial Hornets
come bumbling
out of a
rotten apple,
drunk on
applejack &
staggering.

I can hear
others still
inside, loudly
chewing. There's
little left but
apple skin!

One sits on my
knuckle & grooms
itself like a cat.

FACE-ON!

strong,
chewing
mandibles

yellow & black,
with white
crescent eyes .
yellow legs

Hornet notes. They had completely hollowed the apple and were packed into the empty skin like living stuffing in a pillow!

JOURNAL USES

Your own field journal can be a record of your experiences, providing structure and continuity, or you can use it to study, remember, and understand one of the natural sciences or a particular species. You can record the growth of a tree or a child or the change of seasons, migration patterns, and ecological balances, in both words and pictures.

Use your field journal to record experiments. Remember high-school biology, when we tracked the progress of our test subject against that of a control group? You can do this on your own, and probably with much more interesting results since you choose your own field of study. Do your own comparative analysis studies in your journal. You needn't draw at all if you don't want to; just record whatever interests you, like size, growth rate, or alternate feedings. A small ruler to measure progress and a notebook for your jottings are all you need.

CUP PLANT

Cup Plant heads
(seeds)

Cup plant flowers, leaves, and seed heads.

You can also test theories and hypotheses and record the results in your field journal. Most professional botanists, zoologists, biologists, and others in the natural sciences do. Two journal entries of mine read:

> June 10, 1984: I've read that tansy, the herb, is a good insect repellent. Planted some today. We'll see.
> September 25, 1985—Grasshoppers ate the tansy!

I often find that working in my field journal is a calming, centering experience. It allows me to step outside myself, to get away from stresses and deadlines and *see* what is before me. I can be fully present to the life around me and forget whatever it was that had my shoulders tense and my senses revved up. I slow down. It's as simple as that.

HOW TO SET UP A FIELD JOURNAL

I have been interested in nature as far back as I can remember. I became a *naturalist* when I began keeping a field journal with my own observations, questions, and conclusions. In order to assure a sense of continuity and to keep those records for yourself there are a few simple guidelines I've found it best to follow.

First, use a permanent book. A hardbound book is best for me, since it gets quite a bit of rigorous use. Whatever you choose, use that book continuously until you reach the end, and then start another one: Don't skip around from spiral-bound book to sketchbook to hardbound book. Keeping dated records in sequence makes your journal more useful to you. Date each page as you use it, and add notes about time, temperature (approximate is fine—you don't need to carry a thermometer with you), weather conditions, and any other pertinent facts somewhere on the page. I begin usually at the top since sketches might smear if I rub my hand over them as I work down the page.

As an artist, I tend to design a page. I get pleasure from producing what is called "a nice layout." This is not strictly necessary, of course. Just allow yourself room for sketches and plenty of notes. If you like, make your rough sketches on the left and leave a column on the right for notes and observations. Carry a ruler with you to take measurements and any of your other naturalist's tools to help you keep good notes.

YOUR OWN NATURE TRAIL: CREATION
AND OBSERVATION

Any place may become special to you. One particular area of your city or small-town park might appeal to you for the questions it poses, the curiosity it arouses, its promise of quiet, its special beauty, for its variety of habitats, or animals, or birds. You can use your field journal as a record of areas and events in this one small place, noting separate ecosystems and the things you have seen there or might expect to see at various times of the year.

Look for these areas: transition zones, old-growth forest, climax ecosystems, standing water, moving water, grasslands, open savannas, springs. Look for areas with an abundance of food for various animals and birds, and note which creatures make use of which food sources.

Grasslands and weedy areas have an abundance of seeds. What birds seem to congregate there, and at what season? Old-growth forest will have many standing dead trees and a number of ancient rotting logs, places that are home to billions of burrowing, chewing, boring, or sucking insects, which in their turn attract birds and mammals. Which ones gather near that standing dead elm? Who has made a nest in an old woodpecker's hole? Which mammal's tracks are near the termite nest? Make notes for yourself, and watch. Each of these places or conditions can become a stop on your self-guided nature trail.

When you see a wild animal such as a muskrat, a raccoon, or an opossum, be still and watch it. Note where you saw it and what it was doing. You can be reasonably sure that you are in its home territory and that its den or nest or a favorite feeding area is close by. You may be able to observe the animal again and again in this area at this time of day. Note this in your field journal—location, time, season, what the animal seemed to be doing.

LOOK QUIETLY. Here on the edge of the woods, as on the edge nearly everywhere in nature, there is a stepping up of activity. This is a transition zone. Birds and animals like to feed at the edge of the woods, since the nearby trees offer instant protection: cover from the piercing eyes of predators, and privacy from the prying eyes of humans. I often see a flash of fur or feathers if I approach this area too brazenly, too loudly, too abruptly. In a more contemplative or alert mood I may approach quietly and slowly and see a variety of animals going naturally about their business. If I approach *too* closely, they freeze into unnatural poses, ready to bolt. It's best to be quiet, to carry small field binoculars, or to move under cover and downwind to get as close as possible without losing the subject. This is the first stop on my self-guided nature trail. Taking notes and making sketches of what I see reminds me of what I have seen here before, and I prepare myself for whatever surprises may be waiting for me farther on.

LOOK CLOSELY. As I enter the woods, the path goes steeply upward and then turns and crosses the jumbled rocks of a dry gulch. In times of heavy downpour this rock-strewn gully roars like Niagara in miniature, but

This rocky gulch is a wonderful place to find mushrooms, mosses, and lichens.

mostly it is as it is today—a wonderful, moist spot to look for mosses, mushrooms, and lichen.

A magnificent sorrel bay-colored bowl fungus grew on organic debris there this summer and remained for weeks before it was finally torn apart by squirrels intent on winter stores. The gulch is the next step on my self-guided trail. Here, I always remember to look for any new and different moisture-loving plants, saprophytes, or parasites.

LOOK DOWN. A few feet farther on great trees have fallen and begun their inevitable journey to compost. Insects do their work in breaking down trees that were once giants towering over the tree canopy. Termites, bark beetles, ants, and grubs have made labyrinthine tunnels and turreted castles here. Forests of tiny moss sprout from the always-damp wood fibers, making a home for still more miniature insects. This fall, the largest of these trees was densely dotted with creamy, rounded mushrooms that looked as if they had been lightly browned in the oven. They were soft and pliable to the touch like little buns, and they made a dry, whispery sound when I ran my finger lightly over them. My sketch allowed me to identify them as *Lycoperdon pyriforme,* which are edible when young. I found them in late October, but my mushroom field guide tells me they may be found from early spring to first frosts.

Downy, hairy, and redheaded woodpeckers probe the rotting cellulose for their dinner, looking for all the world as I do when poking around in the refrigerator. In dead summer the mosses may be browned and dried almost beyond recognition, but the first drought breaker will bring them

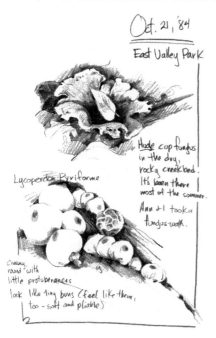

Oct. 21, '84

East Valley Park

Lycoperdon Pyriforme

Huge cup fungus in the dry, rocky creekbed. It's been there most of the summer.

Ann & I took a fungus-walk.

Creamy, round - with little protuberances

look like tiny buns (feel like them, too - soft and pliable.)

My self-guided nature trail always includes a number of fungus sightings in the gulch or on the rotting trees up the hill.

miraculously back to life like the desert after a rain. Within hours they will be lush and green again. In late winter I may be amused and entertained by a flying circus of springtails, those minuscule, prehistoric flealike insects that are the earliest of their relatives to brave the still-frigid winds. A few notes in my field journal reminds me to look for these tiny snow fleas.

LOOK AROUND. Recrossing the gulch higher up, the wonderful colors of the woods always catch my eye. In the spring the hill is covered with spring beauties, Dutchman's-breeches, rue anemones, and wood sorrel. The ground is frosted pink and white with them, and it's difficult to step off the path without crushing their delicate flowers. In summer the sunlight slants through the green canopy overhead, stained-glass windows in a naturalist's cathedral. In fall this same spot glows amber as the young

Springtail (snow flea)

← forked tail

MAGNIFIED "springs" against the ground

Even in winter there is much to see on my trail; if I look closely I will find springtails on the melting snow.

Rue
Anemones
everywhere –
I can't help but
lie on them to
draw this one

Wild flowers grow in profusion up the hill. The area glowed pink with them this spring.

hickories of the understory give up their chlorophyll. They are the first to stop their work of photosynthesis and get on with the autumn—impatient adolescent trees longing to experience life. In the deep woods, where they receive limited sun all summer, their leaves have grown fantastically to compensate for the lack of light; the larger hickories have proportionately normal-sized leaves, but these are often nearly a foot long. When the sun's fingers touch them they are like schools of huge goldfish swimming in the air. Winter colors are subtler, more subdued; all the more precious for being elusive.

LOOK UP. Farther on, the crow tree fills the air with soft mutterings from late spring to fall. Why crows choose this particular tree as a condominium I don't know, but their presence or lack of it makes it a special place for me. So generally raucous and rowdy, these big black birds are fun to watch on their home turf. My sketches here are quick, to catch their fleeting poses as they converse and chatter or look down at me.

LOOK TO YOUR SOURCES. Each stop on my self-guided nature trail has filled my field journal over and over with notes, quick sketches, or studies. When I return home I spend a few minutes—or hours—poring over my "official" field guides, looking for a particular bird, animal, or plant to

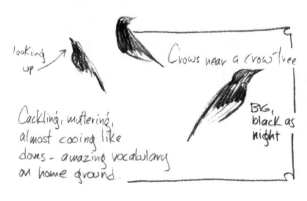

looking
up

Crows near a crow tree

BIG,
black as
night

Cackling, muttering,
almost cooing like
doves – amazing vocabulary
on home ground.

I sketched these crows quickly as I stood beneath their favorite tree. They are normally shy, but I was able to get near enough to at least jot down these rough images.

identify. My ever-growing collection of these guides, on every topic from mushrooms to fossils, allows me to turn my field journal into a personal field guide to a specific area. If I have been careful enough in my observations and notes, and if my sketches are accurate enough (or well-annotated), I can take the things I can't find for myself to a real expert in the field: a biology professor or a geologist at a nearby college or someone in the Missouri Department of Conservation.

GARDEN HAPPENINGS

Your own backyard can fill the pages of your field journal. Who is to say that any other place on earth is more interesting than this small patch of largely unexplored turf?

Perhaps you feel you know it too well or the study would bore you to tears. Try the old trick of marking off a square yard and exploring just there with as much attention as you would a Rocky Mountain pass. Explore it "up close and personal." Use your hand lens. Discover the biology of the place; plants and animals abound, even here. Surprise your piece of turf at midnight or at dawn and note the differences. Remember it in deep winter; what might be surviving there under the snow?

My notebook is full of the comings and goings; births, lives, and deaths of the birds, insects, and animals I live so close to. One winter day I captured the look of surprise on an amazingly large flicker's face as he plastered himself to the screen outside my studio window. We were face to face, not eighteen inches apart; I was as startled as he was, but not too startled to grab my field journal and record his strong, gripping toes and stiff, braced tail feathers. Unless you are lucky enough to be involved in bird banding, the chance doesn't come all that often to see just how big one of these birds really is.

Flicker on my studio window screen. There is a feeder on the window that attracted him.

Your own garden, backyard, or balcony will be full of its own natural happenings. Everywhere the conditions for life are met—and that is virtually everywhere, even on a rooftop in New York City where a pair of kestrels may build their nest—you will have something to see and record. Keep your field journal handy, or carry a small spiral notebook with you at all times. Later, when it is convenient, transfer your rough notes or sketches to your permanent record book.

YOUR BACKYARD WEATHER STATION

We all watch the news on television, waiting to see what the weather is going to be. Will it rain, or how much did it? Should we plan a picnic, or carry an umbrella? How deep was the snow last night, and how cold did it get? How hot *is* it, anyway? Can we expect a change in the weather? It seems over half the time the poor, beleaguered weather reporter is wrong, anyway. At the very least, what he or she reports applies only to the official recording sites.

A backyard weather station returns a sense of control over our own lives, if not the weather itself. We have firsthand knowledge, and we no longer have to depend on what someone "out there" says. We can do this on a daily or weekly basis. Even a simple outdoor thermometer from the hardware store can get you started. Record the temperature in your journal once or twice a day; generally (if you are a morning person) when you first get up and again in the hottest part of the day (most often mid- or late afternoon.) A maximum/minimum thermometer will record these highs and lows for you. This kind of thermometer can be obtained from a hobby store or an outdoor-equipment catalog; or check with your local weather station.

A simple rain gauge can be an inexpensive addition to your home weather station. A dollar or two will buy a plastic version for your garden, patio, or balcony. For accurate readings, remember to place it far enough away from the house or other large objects so it won't be affected by runoff, and dump the water daily so you'll know what each twenty-four-hour period has brought.

Some rain gauges are equipped with a weather vane as well, to tell wind direction and even wind speed. These don't have the charm of the old iron rooster atop the barn, of course, but they are efficient and accessible.

A lovely alternative is a rainbow-colored wind sock mounted on a tree or a pole. All you have to know is where north is in relation to your particular orientation. You can tell the other directions from that.

A barometer is a more expensive addition to your home weather station, but it will let you "tell the future" with some degree of accuracy—concerning weather changes, anyway.

Check out a book on meteorology. Learn to recognize cloud shapes or the effects of high- and low-pressure areas. There are also field guides to the weather. For fun, get a copy of an old farmer's almanac. Notice how accurate weather predictions often are, and when they are wrong.

Sketch clouds, noting what weather conditions were at the time. Be sure to note any changes you observed before or just after sketching the cloud shapes.

All these notations can go into your field journal daily or weekly. They'll serve as a memory jog as you look back over a year. They'll help you know when to expect first frost or a drought breaker, or perhaps when to look for morels in the woods. They'll give you a sense of being grounded on the earth, a part of the changing show of summer and winter and heat and cold and rain.

INSPIRATION AND INSTRUCTION

If you feel inadequate to the task of trying to capture nature on paper, consider a bit of instruction. Take a drawing class, or refer to drawing from nature.*

You can simply trace around a leaf or flower. A very rough sketch will refresh your memory; you needn't think of yourself as an artist to attempt field sketching. Biologists, zoologists, botanists, and others in the natural history fields benefit from even the roughest of images, especially when they are properly annotated with date, time, measurements, and observations, questions, and conclusions.

Never feel that you can't set pencil to paper unless you are a Leonardo. These field sketches are for *your own* pleasure and education. Don't let lack of experience or formal training steal that away from you. Have fun! Enjoy; squiggle down the loosest shape. You will remember. Your own visual aids will act as triggers for your mind.

*See bibliography for specific recommendations.

SEVEN

*Jack-in-the-pulpit or Indian turnip (*Arisaema triphyllum*).*

Wild Flowers and Weeds: Through the Seasons

Finding a jack-in-the-pulpit may be a one-to-a-customer thrill, where you live; or if your climate is hospitable, you may find them by the hundreds. A mild winter followed by a wet-enough spring will fill the woods with them.

I remember the first one I ever found. It was as if I'd found the leprechaun's gold at the end of the rainbow. The jack-in-the-pulpit was alone on a north-facing bank in the woods on our old farm. I had waded the flooded creek to get to the other side and was rewarded by the sun's sending down a single finger of light to point out my treasure. The pulpit glowed like a tiny green lantern; the back light gave it an eerie, lighted-from-within luminosity. I recrossed the creek for my paint box and returned to work while the sun still gave Jack (the spadix) the neon pulpit he deserved. I felt as if I had found a rare, small shred of Shangri-la.

This year the woods are dotted with thousands of them. Now, in September, these same woods are spangled with the scarlet-beaded fruiting head the preacher became, huge and heavy with berrylike seeds. When their season begins to pass, these bright heads on their upright stalks will rot off at the ground and fall to the forest floor to plant their seeds. Inspected closely, the heads are similar to a pomegranate fruit once the hard rind is removed. Individual berries are crowded together on a soft, hollow cone that looks a lot like a small hot pepper, with its cargo of seeds removed. Inside the cone is a white netted membrane. The infinite variety of botanical detail is mind boggling, and the more so when I think that every flower has a unique quality in its seeding, flowering, and fruiting.

Wild flowers are perhaps the second-most-popular reason to go into the wild—bird watching being the first. Their variety and beauty beckon and amaze. Their appearance year after year, season after season, gives us hope, a sense of continuity, and a feeling of order in a sometimes crazy world.

Wild flowers are as beautiful as stationary butterflies. Where you have found them before, in their proper seasons, chances are you will find them again. This is not always true, oddly enough. Whole colonies seem to spring up one year, only to move on like a bright band of gypsies the next. Much depends on growing conditions and weather. As with our jack-in-the-pulpit, the proper growing conditions can make the woods a carpet of colors where one or two may have shyly hidden before. This year everything worked together to make the woods path on my hill a Renaissance tapestry of bloom, crowded with spring beauties, false rue anemones, Dutchman's-breeches, trillium, and bloodroot. Next year a harsh winter or a dry spring might bring only sparsely spaced plants.

The beauty of wild flowers is not there only for our pleasure. Each flower is specially designed to appeal to its particular pollinating insect. Some will not support the weight of a fat bumblebee while others invite the furry visitor deep inside, where pollen may be liberally deposited on its hairy abdomen to be carried conveniently to the next flower. Honeybees are our premier pollinators, of course, and many kinds of wild flowers owe their continued existence to the bee's single-minded search for sustenance to take back to the hive. Where bees have been severely curtailed by too-heavy applications of pesticides, the wild flowers are not the only plants to suffer; crops show a steep decline in productivity.

Even butterflies, flies, and other less familiar insects have their duties to perform as pollinators of flowers that have genetically adapted to just their particular combination of anatomical details (like mouthparts, body shape). There is a symbiotic relationship between these insects and their host flowers. Some flowers develop according to the insects that are available

*Early spring brings this member of the lily family to the park (*Trillium erectum*).*

to pollinate them under particular growing conditions, above the timber-line, for example, or in a desert. Their popularity—or lack of it—with their insect pollinators will deeply affect the form future plant generations will take. You can be sure the necessary adaptations will take place or the flower will soon become extinct. Cross-species pollinations may result in mutations or a whole new type of plant.

APPRECIATING WEEDS

Weeds are nothing more than flowers we haven't yet come to appreci-ate. Many of the weeds we tear out of our manicured lawns are quite beautiful if seen in the right light and without prejudice. The time, ex-pense, and frustration of maintaining a velvet coat of green on my front lawn has never appealed to me, anyway. I enjoy the diversity of my weedy greensward and the variety of bird and insect life it attracts. In this chapter I'll introduce you to my special favorites, some common and some not so common. Some may be your favorites as well. Your own field journal is the place to note and study favorites that I may have ignored. Your gar-den, yard, fence row, or small-town park is the place to look for them.

THE SCIENTIFIC APPROACH

You might prefer a more botanical approach to your study of wild flow-ers. It will certainly help in your identification of species you are unfa-miliar with or with arcane divisions within a species. An understanding of flower parts, such as pistils, stamens, achenes, disks, drupes, and spurs, will add immeasurably to your knowledge of wild flowers. Learning the types of leaves (lobed, toothed, dissected, sessile, pinnately compound, ovate, linear) and flowers (spikes, panicles, umbels, regular, irregular, composite, corymbs, racemes) will help you with identification of a just-discovered but unknown treasure.

A knowledge of flower families will help you find the one you seek in your field guide. For the beginner or weekend naturalist, guides organized by flower color or season are easier to use than ones organized by families. Before you buy, look through the available guides to see which best suits your method of identification.

HARBINGERS OF SPRING

These small, brave flowers signal the end of harsh winter weather. Al-though the wind may still whistle through the bare branches of the trees overhead and ice may form on the puddles, once the first flower has come to inspect the pale sun we know winter has been given its walking papers. It's only a matter of time.

These first wild flowers huddle close to the ground for protection against the changeable weather. Their leaves seem almost translucent and their stems like green thread. Perhaps their rosette of leaves have been seen hugging the ground all winter and the slender stalks rise up like a phoenix from the center as the sun's rays reach high enough in the heavens to set off their internal alarm clock. Many grow from starchy underground bulbs or rhizomes, last year's solar energy having been stored over winter for these first chilly days. They were active underground all winter, forming the embryo of the tender flowers. Cut open a bulb, onionlike and layered, and you will find the spring's plant, leaf, and flower, pale and entire. These are perennials, sprouting from last year's rootstock or bulb or rhizome, rather than from annual seeds; they don't need warm soil to sprout as seeds do. Some mysterious source just seems to call them forth from their long winter sleep, perfectly designed to fulfill their promise.

Here is my own list of spring flowers for my area. I've included family names to help you identify them. Add your own special favorites or locally indigenous flowers to your journal.

RUE ANEMONE. One of the first flowers to bloom in my area, it appears as early as late February (in a particularly kind year) and continues to May. Both rue anemone and false rue anemone (more common in my woods) are members of the buttercup family (Ranunculaceae). Their white flowers and delicate, reddish green stems are very similar, but false rue anemone has deeply lobed compound leaves.

SPRING BEAUTIES. Delicately etched with pink or reddish lines, their pink pollen seems dyed to match. They are members of the purslane family (Portulacaceae), as is the garden plant portulaca and the edible purslane.

April 26, 1984
East Valley Park
hot! + windy

pink veined flower petals
(in the shade they are
darker pink)

about 1½ size

Field journal page. Spring beauty
*(*Claytonia virginica*).*

Dogtooth Violet
(TROUT LILY)
March - April

Dogtooth violet is really a member of the family Liliacae, more commonly called trout lily for its spotted leaves.

We find them from March to May in damp woods and nearby clearings. They range from Ontario to Quebec and New England, south to Georgia, west to Texas, and north to Minnesota. Unless you live in the Rockies and points west, you should find these in the spring.

BLOODROOT. Its reddish green stem is clasped protectively with a capelike single leaf, pale gray-green on the underside. You will find it from March to May in rich leaf mold or along a stream. It belongs to the poppy family (Papaveraceae). Look closely; you can see the resemblance in the flower shape. The bloom itself is pale and as glowing as ivory. The red juice of the underground stem was used by the Indians and the first settlers as a dye. It was even pressed into service as a particularly lurid insect repellent; since it did double duty as war paint, I imagine it repelled more than mosquitoes to be seen on those fearsome red faces!

DOGTOOTH VIOLETS. Their other name, trout lilies, is a much more apt description given their lovely, spotted, fish-shaped leaves. They may be yellow or white (with a reddish blush near the base of the petals) or an allover pink tint if you find the prairie trout lily. Obviously enough—and certainly more obviously than with wild garlic or carrion flower—these are also members of the lily family (Liliaceae). A less well known name for these spring flowers is adder's tongue. The nodding blossom stands at attention as the flowers mature.

JACK-IN-THE-PULPIT. All spring flowers are not delicately colored and tiny. My elusive (or prolific) jack-in-the-pulpit varies from fresh pale green to elegantly striped maroon and green. The large, veined leaves are dull green and divided into three parts. It's a member of the arum family (Araceae), some of which are quite poisonous and others very edible. Hawaiian poi is made from a member of this family. The dichotomy makes for an interesting game of Russian roulette, and one I generally forgo. Green dragon, a very similar plant in growth and leaf, is much rarer. You may find the two growing near each other, as they require similar habitat (moist woods, swamps). The jack may be found from April to June, the dragon a bit later.

Dutchman's-breeches (locally referred to as "britches") are closely related to squirrel corn and wild bleeding heart.

DUTCHMAN'S-BREECHES. My favorite of the early spring flowers, they are tiny white pantaloons sometimes subtly striated with pale pink, looking for all the world as if they'd been hung out to dry on a fairy's clothesline. They have deeply cut, lacy gray-green leaflets that are a headache to draw but a pleasure to look at. They have a wonderfully broad range, from North Dakota and beyond as well as all points east and north to Nova Scotia and Quebec—everyman's messenger of spring. Closely related are the wild bleeding heart and the pale, heart-shaped squirrel corn. They are all members of the poppy family (as is bloodroot).

WILD GINGER. Later in the spring, other wild flowers appear. This plant is unique. With red-brown petals with a fuzzy white back, it looks as if it couldn't quite decide whether to be a flower or a small, furry animal. It is a member of the birthwort family (Aristolochiaceae). You may miss this little flower altogether; like the shy forest creature it resembles, it tends to hide beneath the cover of large, hairy leaves that may be six inches wide. It's earned its name: The strong, gingerlike flavor works well as a substitute when sweetened with sugar. Look under those broad green umbrellas in April and May.

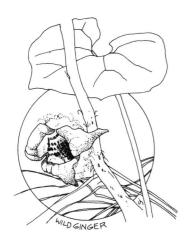

Furry, brown wild ginger hiding under broad leaves.

Perfoliate bellwort (Uvularia perfoliata) *is very similar to wild oats.*

WILD OATS. You don't have to sow your wild oats to find them blooming happily away for you. This lily family (Liliaceae) member is also called sessile bellwort, and the drooping yellow flowers resemble bells more than they do oats. This summer I found the foliage of a near relative, perfoliate bellwort. The stem seemed to have been threaded through the leaves the way I used to sew leaves together with sticks as a child. You may find these blooming until June in some locations, and as early as April. They have a broad range as well.

MAY APPLES. They have such showy, shiny green leaves that you may not have realized they harbor a nodding, waxy white flower. I noticed this spring, as I looked for some to draw, that only the plants with a crotch, two stems, and two leaves had flowers. Single stalks produced no flower. Later in the season the flower becomes a lemonlike fruit from which some people have made quite passable jam. This plant is also called a mandrake, but it is not related to the European plant of the same name. The roots, leaves, and seeds are all poisonous if eaten in large quantities. It is a member of the barberry family (Berberidaceae).

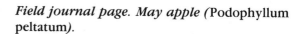

*Field journal page. May apple (*Podophyllum peltatum*).*

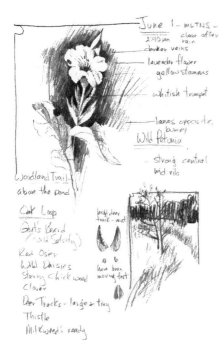

Field journal page. Wild flowers.

VIOLETS. Last in my list of favorite spring flowers is one I share with many as a symbol of spring. Violets have even found their way onto greeting cards and into the local florist shop. *Missouri Wildflowers** lists sixteen common violets, not counting the dogtooth (trout lily). Peterson lists thirty-nine, and the Audubon guide says that there are "about 22 genera and 900 species found nearly throughout the world," making this one of the most accessible of spring flowers. You may find not only my favorite, bicolored bird's-foot violets, but also yellow, white, and blue ones of all sizes. The green violet is hard to recognize as such, but it is a member of the (Violaceae) family in good standing nonetheless.

SUMMER'S BOUNTY

For a few weeks in June, it seems as if there are only a few wild flowers blooming. The great explosion of spring has passed, and the small woods flowers have faded in the dense shade of the leafed-out forest or been strangled in the tall grasses by the road. Be patient, however. In a week or two, summer's bounty will come in, and the fields and hills will be a calico quilt of bloom.

Summer's flowers are often showy, robust, and tall to reach toward the light. Competition is keen, and the delicate, tiny flowers of spring wouldn't stand a chance. The edge of the woods is dressed in a sprigged fabric of flower colors and shapes. A whole field may suddenly blush golden or

*Denison Edgar, *Missouri Wildflowers.* Jefferson City, Mo.: Missouri Department of Conservation, 1972. See bibliography for other field guides to wild flowers.

blue as a stand of summer flowers comes into season. In some parts of the country, where purple loosestrife has escaped and spread to become a threat to the indigenous flowers and plants, the fields, backyards, and vacant lots are as purple as if they had been painted with a brush. Roadsides are edged in tender sky blue as chickory opens its morning flowers to the day. Other places are a low mat of buttery yellow where bird's-foot trefoil has spread. I feel like Dorothy following the yellow brick road to Oz. Day lilies grow in great clumps of orange along the roads, in old farmsteads, and in our park. Wild roses fill the air with their scent, competing with Japanese honeysuckle for sheer sweetness and for space as well. The honeysuckle has escaped cultivation like the loosestrife and has strangled whole stands of trees in its enthusiasm. Many of my favorites are summer flowers that grow near water, perhaps because in summer I am drawn to the active environment that water affords. There is so much to see: turtles, frogs, crayfish, toads, fish, mammals that make the water their home or come here to drink, birds that fish for their dinner or simply come to bathe, the metallic gleam of dragonflies and damselflies, and the antics of water striders and whirligig beetles. There is always something to find—including flowers that bloom in or near water. Here is my list of summer flowers. Add others, if you like, to your own field journal.

WATER WILLOW. A low-growing plant, it looks little like a willow tree except in its narrow, lanceolate leaves. Mats of them, growing closely together, form grassy islands in my creek in summer. Look closely at the flowers. They are as exotic as orchids, although they are members of the acanthus family (Acanthaceae). They are odd-shaped flowers, with their white throats dotted with purple. Anthers are purplish red, and the upper lip may be pale violet. It's an elegant, small flower, to be found from June to October.

SMARTWEED OR KNOTWEED. Both plants have deep pink miniature flowers that often look like never-opening buds. Smartweeds have flowers in terminal spikes, while the knotweeds have flower clusters in leaf axils. Lady's thumb, another member of the buckwheat family (Polygonaceae) has a dark imprint on the lanceolate leaves (apparently where "Our Lady" has left her mark). These flowers can all be found near water, in old fields, and in damp waste places, from May to October.

JEWELWEED. Along our creek, near the fishing lake at Rocky Hollow and at the shady edge of the woods, this plant hangs its brilliant orange and golden flowers on translucent stems. Spotted touch-me-not, also a jewel-weed, has reddish brown spots. These are members of the touch-me-not family (Balsaminaceae), which includes the familiar garden impatiens. The fire-bright colors and ornate shapes explain their common name, but the origin of the touch-me-not appellation is more fun to discover. In late

Pale touch-me-not or jewelweed
(Impatiens pallida).

summer or fall when the seedpods have formed, look quickly—when touched they explode to disperse their small seeds. The sides of the seed capsules curl instantly to loose the seeds. Share this phenomena with a child to initiate him or her into the wonders of nature.

AMERICAN LOTUS. Also called water chinaquin, it may completely cover the surface of a shallow pond or a slow-moving stream. At a nearby wildlife sanctuary, the oxbow lakes formed by the changing of the channel of the Missouri River are nearly choked with them, making a spectacular midsummer habitat for catfish, frogs, rails, gallinules, great blue herons, and cattle egrets.

The waxy yellow flowers are huge and followed by seedpods that look for all the world like wasps' nests carved in wood. Each indentation holds a round seed, supposed to be edible. The leaves are like dinner platters and may rise three feet above the surface of the water. These flowers belong to the water lily family (Nymphaeaceae).

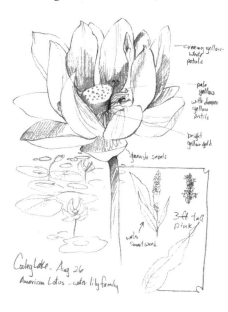

*Field journal page. American lotus; smartweed (*Nelumbo lutea; Polygonum coccineum).

LILIES. These are well represented among summer's flowers. Besides the lovely orange day lilies, look for the more exotic Turk's-cap lily. The recurved petals of these drooping orange flowers are spotted with reddish brown and grow at the tops of tall (from three to seven inches) stems. They like wet meadows and the edge of the woods. You might also find them in swampy areas. It is a member of the lily family (Liliaceae).

STARRY CAMPION. This plant takes on various forms according to growing conditions and available light. Usually you will find the white flowers clustered on tall, slender stalks in open woods. The first one I found was in deep woods and had only a single flower. The sepals are distinctively bell shaped and seem to clasp the petals loosely. As members of the pink family (Caryophyllaceae) they have relatives that range from the corn cockle to the showy fire pink to the common chickweed.

BUTTERFLY WEED. It's the show-off of the milkweed family (Asclepiadaceae). Its small flowers cluster in knock-'em-dead orange. You can't miss it on roadsides or open fields. It seems to thrive on dry conditions and is often seen in the rocky Missouri Ozarks. The Indians chewed the root for pleurisy and other diseases of the lungs, hence its other name: pleurisy root.

BUTTERCUPS. The polished petals are unmistakable, no matter which family member you find. The kidney-leaf buttercup has tiny yellow petals, but they are as shiny as if they had been lacquered, as are the petals of the bulbous buttercup, the swamp buttercup, and the common buttercup. Like the rue anemone, these are members of the buttercup family (Ranunculaceae) and may be found in your yard and garden. The swamp buttercup, despite its name, can also be found in thickets and moist woods. Some member of the group can be found from April to September.

A somewhat atypical starry campion (Silene stellata)*; these flowers are usually clustered on slender stalks. This deep-woods specimen simply didn't get enough light to produce more than a single flower.*

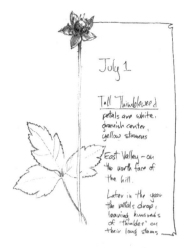

*Thimbleweed study (*Anemone virginiana*).*

TALL THIMBLEWEED. This is another member of the buttercup family. The mature seedlike pistils gives this flower its name. The green head is quite thimblelike in size and shape. You may find it from June until August in rocky woods and dry places. Its flowers are white, but they still bear a strong family resemblance to its shiny yellow cousins.

SMALLER PUSSYTOES. One of my favorite strange little flowers is smaller pussytoes. They look just like their namesakes. The flowers are small, rounded, fuzzy white "toes" clustered at the end of a woolly stem. I guarantee you will laugh the first time you see one; they're just plain cute. Oddly enough, this is a member of the sunflower family (Compositae, formerly Asteraceae), which it resembles not at all. Look for it and plantain-leaved pussytoes from May to July in pastures and open woods. I found my first one near an old, abandoned one-room schoolhouse.

INDIAN PIPE. Another odd flower with a decidedly otherworldly feel it is pale, ghostly, and saprophytic. These white flowers have no chlorophyll at all. The leaves are reduced to scales closely hugging the erect stem. You'll find them growing in a friendly relationship with fungus in damp leaf mold. Look for them from June to September. I found my first in an area where three-wheeled off-road vehicles had knocked them into the path in the woods on a north-facing hill. A close relative is the pinesap, which may have yellow, red, pink, or even lavender flowers—but not green leaves, since it is also saprophytic. These are members of the Indian pipe family (Monotropaceae). I took my Indian pipes home, where they turned a deathlike black in the course of a week.

QUEEN ANNE'S LACE. No mention of summer flowers would be complete without Queen Anne's lace, which often grows in such profusion near day lilies and thistles as to make them seem to have a symbiotic relationship.

Delicate and lacy, the broad heads made up of hundreds of miniature flowers form white umbrellas that turn to tiny woven baskets as their season passes. You may see them all winter as curled, lacy brown heads, perhaps filled with snow. Also called wild carrot, this is a member of the parsley family (Apiaceae).

BRAVE STRAGGLERS

You might find the flowers listed here much earlier in the summer, but their hardy nature allows them to be among the last to bloom, prolonging summer's beauty until after first frost or longer. These hardy late bloomers include the asters and many of the sunflowers. In fact, the Indians called September "The Month the Yellow Flowers Bloom." Look to see which flowers are still about in September, October, and even November. Since some early spring flowers show their faces as early as February in many areas, very little of the year is without some sort of flowering plant to see or seek. Here are my favorite late-blooming flowers.

ASTERS. They are everywhere in the fall. Calico asters, New York asters, tansyleaf asters, ironweed's purple heads—they debut in August and close the show only when dead winter turns them to dried, skeletal bouquets

Field journal page. Late wild flowers.

of subtle beige and wheat. Some are up to six feet tall, with thousands of small, daisylike flower heads; others grow no more than six inches in their chosen sandy soil. They like waste places, open fields, roadsides, prairies, and limestone banks. In September it seems that any place you look you will see these members of the composite family (Compositae).

THISTLES. The bane of a farmer's existence, their prickly good looks always make me smile—as long as I don't have to try to eradicate them from my garden or step on them barefoot. These plants look as if they could take on an army and win. They are closely related to the spineless asters and are also members of the composite family.

TEASELS. With their spiny stems and prickly flower heads, they look as if they should be related to thistles, but they are not. They're members of the teasel family (Dipsacaceae) itself. Interestingly, these spiked flower-head "pincushions" are still used to comb wool. Their culture was once an important industry in this country.

SUNFLOWERS. These golden flowers and their kin brighten roadsides and fields throughout late summer and fall. Black-eyed Susans, brown-eyed Susans, coneflowers, and sneezeweed all have distinctive dark centers, very much like a dark, sprightly "eye" of disk florets in the middle of the yellow rays of their composite flower heads. Green-headed and gray-headed coneflowers have centers to match their names, but most other members of the sunflower family have pale tan or yellow centers. I find them in the park near the creek or at the edge of the woods. Like asters, they belong to the composite family.

GOLDENROD. It has gotten bad press from hay fever sufferers, but it's a bum rap—actually, the culprit is the much more inconspicuously flowering ragweed. Pollen grains of goldenrod are too large to be airborne for very long distances. You can safely pick them in your backyard or park for an autumn bouquet. Peterson lists twenty-nine varieties of goldenrod. The familiar plumelike shape isn't the only form goldenrod takes. It may be flat topped, elm branched, slender, or clublike. As different in looks from asters or sunflowers as one could imagine, they are still members of the same family. Look for these variations from July through October.

SPURGES. Look for snow-on-the-mountain until October. These showy green-and-white "flowers" are really bracts. The actual flowers are the tiny, knotlike centers. This shrubby plant is a Euphorbiaceae family member. While you look for it in the open areas, keep an eye out for a plant suspiciously similar to a Christmas poinsettia but without the pink, white, or red bracts. Wild poinsettia, also a spurge, grows in sandy soil and in open or wooded areas. Near the characteristic poinsettialike centers, the bracts may have a bit of white or red that gives them away but are mostly a solid green.

*Rough-stemmed goldenrod (*Solidago rugosa*).*

WHEN WINTER COMES . . .

Don't think the beauty of wild flowers has left the woods, the park, or the borders of your backyard until next spring just because the blooming season has passed. Many of these plants make fascinating, elegant pods or dried seed heads, just right for an autumn or winter bouquet. Look especially for the pods of milkweed, pennycress, thistle, goldenrod, Queen Anne's lace, teasel, campion, ironweed, and even those ubiquitous asters. Your careful observations throughout the year plus your field journal notes will help you to identify which pod or seed head is the result of which plant. Some plants need to be harvested as soon as they form their pods, since they shatter once winter winds blow or snow weights them down, so look for shepherd's purse, pennycress, and peppergrass pods in early summer.

WILD-FLOWER GARDEN

You can grow many of these wild beauties right in your own backyard, or even in planters on a city balcony. First, you might try letting nature take its course in a selected corner of your yard. See what volunteers; then if you like what you see, encourage growth by weeding and watering. We have had many nice surprises even here in our small-town garden. The wild poinsettia of the patio is only one of many.

Look at what grows in the wild under similar conditions to those found in your yard. There is no use hoping for swamp milkweed or water willow if your yard is as dry as the Sahara; conversely, a boggy yard is not the place to plant a prairie mix. You only cause yourself more maintenance problems than anyone should have to cope with if you go against nature. If your yard is shady, with deep topsoil or lots of leaf mold, the early spring wild flowers of the forest should flourish there. If you have an open field for a front yard, asters, sunflowers, and gayfeather should fare well.

Make a rock garden of a stony place. You can look to see what grows naturally in such places in the wild.

Many flowers in their native habitat are near extinction or on the endangered species list. Others are simply difficult to transplant from the wild, and so your work and their lives would be wasted. Buy seed, plants, or rootstock from a reputable dealer. *Do not* go into the wild or even your corner park with a shovel. Many of these places are protected by law, and you could be liable for a heavy fine.

leaves found
by the creek:
oaks, elm,
sycamore, walnut, sumac,
buckeye, linden, etc.

Late fall leaves.

Trees: The Green Giants

Reaching deep into the earth, searching for moisture and seeking nutrients in the form of inorganic salts, trees are our largest living plants. With limbs outstretched to the sky, dancing with the wind, they perform mysterious magic with the air (a leafy legerdemain), exchanging oxygen for the miracles of photosynthesis. They turn carbon dioxide, inorganic salts, and water into soluble plant food. Then, as if bored with the game, they shut down the magic act one chilly night when the light has been just right and transform green robes to gold and orange and scarlet.

TREE FORMS

These towering plants are everywhere except in the driest of deserts or above the timberline. Our backyards and parks are full of them, just waiting to be studied and observed through the seasons. I like to choose a tree to study throughout the passing months: the bare tree in winter with its inky, spidery branches; the new buds or flowers; the tree form in full summer; bark patterns; fruit or nuts—and the animals, birds, and insects that make it home. I may even document the tree's demise and gradual return to earth if I am able to sustain the relationship long enough.

As we look and *see*, we realize the wonderful variety of the shapes and

The field journal page is a study of many phases in a walnut tree's life.

forms of trees. Consider the Lombardy poplar's graceful spire, the oak's gnarled form, willow's weak, wandlike limbs that disguise its resilient strength, sycamore's ghostly limbs. There are tremendous distinctions even within a single species. Environmental factors such as available nutrients, moisture, and position in the forest affect the final shape. A tree deep in the woods, competing for space and light, can reach twenty feet or more without ever making a side branch. The same tree in the open may look very much like that child's lollipop, if it is a sugar maple; an urnlike shape if it is an elm; or a conical pin oak form.

Environmental factors such as available light may make a tree take a less-than-characteristic shape. Here a tree, once deep in a forest, shows the effects of competition for sun.

The structure of roots forms a firm foundation for the visible crown as well as drawing moisture and nutrients from the soil.

ADAPTABLE SURVIVORS

A tree is an amazing organism. The sheer size is a mind boggler—especially when you consider that the finest roots often extend as deep into the earth as the crown pierces the sky. The root system, as a general rule, reaches as far (or farther) laterally underground as the width of the visible branches. It is almost as if there are two trees, existing side by side in two realities: the visible tree, the tree we know, and its mirror image upside down in the soil.

Everyone knows that you can tell a tree's age by counting the concentric growth rings when the tree is cut, but it is amazing to think we can also read the earth's story there. Droughts, storms, and fires leave their mark. A year of abundant rain and burgeoning growth or a parched season of almost no growth are easily read in the history book of living wood.

Trees are incredibly adaptable. They are *survivors*. Only human beings, a violent storm, an inferno of forest fire, a blast of lightning, or a family of diligent beavers will kill a tree outright. A slower death resulting from injury, infection, or disease might take several seasons (or even years), but often the tree overcomes, heals itself, and lives. Growth rings tell this tale, too. If the nutrient-carrying phloem layer remains largely intact, the tree will live. A forest fire may blacken a ring, a diseased limb may be shed, or a hungry porcupine may threaten to girdle the trunk and cut off the life-giving nutrients, but the tree survives and heals over the wound, leaving a visible scar.

Even under the harshest conditions trees have managed to adapt and survive. A tree under optimum conditions may grow rapidly, straight, and tall. Clinging to the arid rocks of a canyon wall the same tree will grow slowly, gnarled by the wind and lack of available nutrients, but it will survive. One ancient, twisted bristlecone pine (*Pinus aristata*) in California is believed to be over four thousand years old.

TREE "PERSONALITIES"

Learn the "personality" of the various kinds of trees. This may sound anthropomorphic (and perhaps it is), but it helps make our study an enjoyable one. Notice which trees in your park or backyard are able to withstand a storm. The oaks might be almost unshaken, while the walnuts, surprisingly, lose many of their smaller limbs. Any night we have a good windstorm we can expect a free supply of kindling wood from our neighbor's silver maple (*Acer saccharinum*).

Subjectively speaking, some trees may give us a comforting sense of perseverance, of strength; others, like a small sprout growing from a cut giant, speak of hope and regeneration. That California bristlecone makes me feel that perhaps, after all, we may survive the nuclear age and the pollution we've brought on ourselves.

TREES IN COMMUNITY

Home for myriad creatures from raccoons to pileated woodpeckers to bark beetles, trees are fascinating to study as ecosystems unto themselves. Many birds and small animals will make their homes in these forest giants.

Often a new tree will sprout from a cut trunk, gradually reforesting a cut-over area.

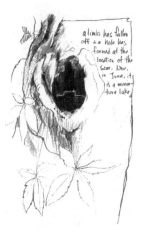

a limb has fallen off + a hole has formed at the location of the scar. Now, in June, it is a miniature lake.

A hole may form once a limb has fallen; this small pool of water is a breeding ground for mosquito larvae.

Some of these creatures seem to prefer a particular species of tree, perhaps for availability of a chosen food source, perhaps for the quality of the wood. Silkworms exist almost exclusively on mulberry trees. Bark beetles often take their name from the type of tree they prefer (European elm, hickory, pine, or spruce bark beetles).

Observe a tree's interwoven web of life. A branch may rot and fall off, leaving a wound that also will rot. A woodpecker may come to enlarge the hole for a nest or in search of food. Later, a squirrel or a bluebird may move into the vacant hole.

Pigeons nest in the hollow trunk of my neighbor's maple. Above a rotted branch stump, an immense shelf fungus has begun its work of slowly digesting the dead or dying wood. The squirrels may find this saprophyte to be a tasty meal later in the winter. The tallest branches have been a motel for traveling bands of redwing blackbirds in the spring and fall, and the fully leafed crown has provided nesting sites all summer long for a variety of small perching birds.

Even after death, when the tree lies at last on the forest floor, it continues to nourish and provide a home for small creatures. In the "slow combustion of decay," the stored solar energy of the decades is burned invisibly on the earth. Mushrooms, mosses, and lichens digest the tree's fibers. Ants and termites burrow and nest and feast. Microorganisms find sustenance in the rotting wood, and soon (in ten or fifty years), depending on moisture conditions, all traces of the tree beyond a changed soil chemistry on the forest floor are gone; earth to earth, the cycle complete.

STORED ENERGY

A tree we have cut for our hearth releases the sun's energy more visibly. That's many years of stored sunlight we feel warming our bones on a cold winter night. (Even oil and coal are the residue of prehistoric trees.)

A wood fire produces more than a cozy feeling. The warm glow means that water is evaporating. Wood is breaking down chemically into charcoal, gas, and volatile liquids. No wonder the fire pops and crackles—a lot is going on! Carbon dioxide is a by-product of this process. Perhaps the same carbon dioxide will later be a part of another tree's process of photosynthesis. Another cycle is complete.

Do you automatically think of the evergreen softwoods as being poor fuel trees and the deciduous hardwoods (those trees that lose their leaves in the fall) as superior? It's not always so. Study any chart of relative British Thermal Units (BTUs) in the various woods (you can find this in any discussion of wood as a fuel source), and you may be in for a surprise or two. Deciduous basswood, at 14.7 million BTUs, makes a poor showing against shortleaf pine's (*Pinus echinata*) 19.0 million. Osage orange (*Maclura pomifera*) recognizable in the fall when it is decorated with the huge, convoluted pale green Christmas ornaments called "hedge apples," is a very hard, dense wood, packing 30.7 million BTUs into a cord of dry wood. Also deciduous, cottonwood (poplar family) has only a 16.1 million rating. Aspens and yellow poplars (both poplar family) are poor fuel woods, deciduous or not; even the evergreen eastern red cedar (*Juniperus virginiana*) gets a better rating from the USDA.

Wood density and moisture levels are the deciding factors for good fuel wood, not whether or not a tree is deciduous.

GYMNOSPERMS AND ANGIOSPERMS

A scientific classification of trees divides them into gymnosperms and angiosperms: those trees that produce fruits without the necessity of flowering first, and those that flower before fruiting.

Gymnosperms such as pines often bear their fruits in protective scales, others in a fleshy cup (yew family), in a "berry" (cedar or cypress family), or in a drupaceous form (like the nonnative ginkgo).

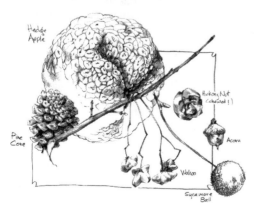

Field journal page. Fall "fruits."

Silver
Maple
leaf rubbing

Leaf rubbing done with a soft black litho crayon.

Angiosperms, perhaps more familiar to the amateur naturalist, do pro-duce flowers. Their seeds are formed within a closed vessel, sometimes fleshy. Think of the nuts, pawpaws, apples, plums, or cherries. Also in-cluded in this classification are members of the legume family (locusts, redbuds), hollies, sumacs, and even the deciduous spurges (oysterwood, manchineel). Bittersweet, that woody vine with berrylike bright orange fruits so symbolic of autumn, has members that cross over to the classifi-cation of trees—think of the eastern wahoo (spindleberry, in Britain).

LEAF SHAPES

When we were children, we collected leaves to study in school, and unless we have wanted a bright fall centerpiece most of us haven't thought of it since. Go into the woods anytime after the trees have leafed out and pick up as many shapes as you can find. Draw them, dry them, trace around them, or make rubbings, but make yourself a permanent record of the diversity of the forest community where you live. The Missouri Ozarks are largely clothed with oak/hickory forests, with a variety of smaller trees like redbud, dogwood, sassafras, and serviceberry claiming space in the understory. In eastern forests, you will find sugar maple, yellow birch, yellow poplar, sweetgum, and the basswoods.

July, late

Immature
bur oak
acorn - green, still

Field journal sketch. Acorn.

In the boreal forest, which covers most of Canada, Alaska, and the area near Lake Superior, parts of Michigan, Minnesota, and Wisconsin, and suitably cool elevations in the Appalachians as far south as Georgia, you will find spruce, jack pine, and fir, mixed in some areas with quaking aspen, paper birch, and balsam poplar.

In mountainous areas, evergreen-aspen forests will predominate. Near a water source, the forest community may alter to reflect a difference in habitat. Cottonwoods, sycamores, willows, and other water-loving trees will take their place beside the more drought-tolerant species.

Your leaf collection should be fully annotated as to where you found each leaf (or evergreen needle or bundle), the conditions it was growing under, position in the forest (the edge or deep inside), season, and size of tree. You will notice that often the smallest trees of a particular species— the saplings—will sport the biggest leaves; it's comical at first, but also very practical. These smaller trees must store and convert energy for growth and they make up for their relative poverty in numbers of leaves through size. Notice, if it is early in the season, that these youngsters will have leafed out first to get a head start. Later, when their fully leafed elders have shaded them, they will have collected sufficient energy to carry them through to the following season. They may begin to drop their leaves as early as July.

Your leaf notes will tell you much about growing conditions and the diversity of wildlife you may expect to see in your park or backyard. An oak-hickory forest may support an incredible number of nut-loving squirrels, for instance, but in the forest depths few rabbits or deer can be found. These animals prefer the convenient cover that the forest edge near a transition zone offers for its availability to preferred foodstuffs. Some of your leaves will show insect damage from feeding or nest building. Try to identify the galls that dot the backs of oak or box elder (*Acer negundo*) leaves. Notice that tent caterpillars tend to favor certain trees, redbuds among them. Some leaves will be curled and misshapen; a caterpillar has made a home here. Take the leaf home and put it in a screen-covered jar to see what emerges.

an empty chrysalis -
the creature formed himself
a cozy nest of
maple keys

Insect chrysalis in maple keys.

Some of your leaves will be fuzzy, almost velvety on the underside (the sycamores), while others will have the look of fine, polished leather (oaks). Some will feel thin and tender, and others, like the plains cottonwood's heart-shaped leaves, will feel stiff as a manila file folder. Some will be tiny and grow in fernlike fronds (locusts, walnuts, and ailanthus family members). Others will be big as a dinner plate.

Use these differences to spark your curiosity. Ask yourself questions: How does this particular tree make use of the available nutrients? How does photosynthesis occur? Why does it grow in association with other species? What protection does it have from insect predators? How did it evolve this particular shape, and why? Use your field guides to help you find the answers.

LIGHT TRICKS

Warm, sunny days and cool nights are the cause of the autumn pyrotechnics in all deciduous trees. Jack Frost has nothing to do with it (just the opposite, in fact: A hard freeze kills the leaves in the forest just as it does the plants left unprotected on your front porch. If the thermometer drops below freezing, leaves that were brilliant with color only yesterday will look blasted and burned, drained of their lighted-from-within pigmentation).

When the daylight and the temperature variances are just right, the leaves form a cutaneous layer of cells between the stem and the leaf. This thick abscission layer will allow the leaf to fall without damage to the tree or without leaving an open wound to become infected later. Sugars, the carbohydrate-based plant food formed in photosynthesis, can't pass out of the leaf as readily as before through this thicker layer of cells and are trapped. Through some natural magic they are transformed into pigments. The woods explode with color. The varied leaf structures in different trees accounts for the fact that some turn as soon as the nights begin to cool while others are still brilliant when the rest of the forest is bare.

Oxygen is the by-product of this summer-long photosynthesis. Trees produce nearly all the oxygen we breathe. Is it any wonder environmentalists express concern over the effects of acid rain, slash-and-burn agricultural practices, and overlogging? Not only is the fragile forest ecosystem disrupted but also the very air we breathe may eventually be changed beyond repair. The nuclear winter theory speaks to this concern as well: Without enough light the trees will not be able to perform their benign magic.

BARK PATTERNS

As well as leaf shapes and flower or seed forms, bark is a very real aid to tree identification. This dead, corky layer protects and insulates the nutrient-rich cambium layer from extremes of heat and cold and sudden

Distinctive sycamore bark is very different close to the ground and on the upper limbs.

impacts. Each tree species seems to do it differently. Any good field guide will include drawings or photos of bark configurations; like a map, these hints and signs will help you know your park's trees. Begin, if you like, with the easiest to recognize: shagbark hickory, eastern red cedar, paper birch, sycamores. Soon you'll be able to discern the variety of oaks by the bark alone.

DEFENSIVE MEASURES

Don't think that because a tree stands there, relatively immobile, that it is defenseless against attacks by predators. Many have evolved quite effective evasive techniques. Look at the thorns of the locust trees, many of the hawthorns, and the honey locust (*Gleditsia triacanthos*). I measured a single thorn once that was almost fourteen inches long—quite a defense mechanism.

Many leaves have protective devices. Hairy, prickly surfaces are hard to walk over if you are a small caterpillar. The serrated edges of many leaves perform the same function. Look closely at the margins of elm leaves, and imagine what it would be like to pull yourself along that endless flight of stairs.

Other trees are more subtle in their defenses. Notice early in the year, when oak leaves may be under attack by oak leaf skeletonizers. You may find leaves that have prematurely fallen to the forest floor. Pick one up and examine it closely. The "meat" of the leaf—the tenderest cells—have been eaten away by tiny caterpillars, leaving only the lacy skeleton.

The oak, like many trees, spreads its canopy quickly to start photosynthesis. The first young leaves are unprotected, and a tree may lose up to seven percent of its total leaf production to the hordes of hungry insects that attack such a succulent salad. Once it is well leafed out, however, the tree can turn its energy to protection, and the chemical war is on. The oak tree musters its defenses and surrounds each hole in its leaves with a powerful chemical. Next the whole leaf is infused with this natural insecticide, then the twig system nearby. Finally the entire tree becomes deadly to the small, gnawing predators. They will die, become deformed, or simply starve to death if they don't move on.

Some trees, especially the alders, seem to have a sophisticated system of communication, a kind of early warning system for trees. Within hours of the first attack all the trees of the same species downwind are busily producing their own chemical insecticides.

Some trees form beneficial and symbiotic relationships with certain insects, notably ants. These fierce defenders patrol entire trees on the lookout for edible insects such as caterpillars and aphids. A tree may reward the ant population for its services with nectar and get pollinated into the bargain. Trees without such a resident army are much more subject to depredations.

FORETASTES AND ECHOES

Look at the woods in early spring before the first tender green appears. The protective sheaths of the buds swell. They glow in shades of red, purple, warm brown, and sienna orange, as a taste of fall color in early spring.

Look again in late fall when most of the leaves lie, toast colored, on the forest floor. A few trees, mostly the water lovers, retain their soft pale green leaves. Willows and the tallest twigs of sycamore shine against the browns of the bare forest. The grass is often still green, not yet nipped by hard winter. The feeling is one of spring, an echo in your mind.

Once the winter cold has passed, a very real foretaste of the season to come is there if we look closely enough. On winter's bare twigs the buds of next spring's leaves are already formed. The buds make the tree as recognizable as its leaves or bark do. Add these notes to your field journal and you will be well on your way to recognizing trees in all seasons.

SEED SNOW

From early spring until fall you may see tree seeds as thick as a January snowstorm falling from the sky. My garden was carpeted with them this spring—a seed mulch. Many sprouted in the moist fertile soil, but of those I had missed with my hoe, almost all had died or succumbed to hungry squirrels by fall. As everywhere in nature, survival of the fittest applied here in my own backyard.

Maple keys (seed pairs) spiral festively, like a fleet of toy helicopters. The smaller seeds drop like tiny buds. Watch to see how nature has outfitted these small capsules of life for distributing themselves to a hospitable habitat. Various members of the maple family produce seeds successively, each in its turn. A single seed pair (key) may travel great distances if the wind is right or if carried by a stream.

Some tree seeds will be eaten by mammals and may pass unharmed through the digestive tract to be planted far from the parent tree. Other smaller seeds are enclosed in a translucent envelope, fringed for aerodynamic lift. I love to watch the parachuting seeds of members of the linden family like American basswood. A specialized "leaf," much different from the characteristic leaf form that makes up the largest part of the canopy, carries the linden seeds to earth. This leaflike bract is slender and ovate, not toothed and heart shaped like the larger (actual) leaves of these basswoods. A stemlike stalk grows from the midrib, carrying first the creamy white flowers, and then the nutlike fruits.

Watch for tree seeds in season. They are as distinctive as any other of the diagnostic hints you may find in the forest or in your backyard.

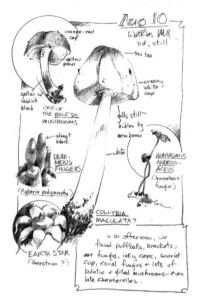

NINE

In the field journal:
Aug 10
Watkins Mill
Hot, still
—fan tan

orange-red cap
yellow pores
yellow or reddish blush
ONE OF THE BOLETUS MUSHROOMS
—almost black.
DEAD MENS FINGERS
(Xylaria polymorpha)
EARTH STAR (Geastrum ?)
—creamy white cap
gills still hidden by membrane
—white
MARASMIUS ANDROSACEUS (horsehair fungus)
COLLYBIA MACULATA?

In an afternoon, we found puffballs, brackets, ear fungus, inky caps, scarlet cup, coral fungus + lots of boletus + gilled mushrooms—even late chanterelles.

Field journal page.
Mushroom varieties.

Mushrooms, Lichens, and Mosses

The world at our feet is not the habitat of wild flowers and tree roots alone. It is also a mysterious realm of nonflowering plants going about their business of growing and reproducing in ways we might not have guessed. That mushroom sprouting from a dead log needs no chlorophyll at all. It works no miracles of photosynthesis and grows as well at night as in the light of day. Its alchemy is beneficial to us. As a saprophyte, it helps to break down and release the chemical and organic compounds bound up in leaf mold, dead and dying trees, and other plants and returns them to simpler forms so they may be used by others. The cycle is perfect and complete.

Lichens are slow-growing, sturdy plants, perhaps pre-dating the seed-growing plants by millions of years. They are pioneers; hardy and adventurous, they grow where other plants cannot. The arctic tundra supports many kinds of lichen. Theoretically, these same plants would be able to survive on the scorching surface of the red planet, Mars—in fact some scientists speculate that Mars's reddish color may be attributable to lichen or some similar life form.

Mosses soften the harsh contours of damp rocks and cover the moist places with velvet beards. Like mushrooms and lichen, they also work to break down dead wood and debris and return the elements to their simpler chemical compounds. In midsummer drought they may look as dead

brown
w/black
(spores?
spore cases?)
tiny
"mystery fungus"
on a walnut tree's
bark — 50X mag. —
couldn't see it
at all with the naked
eye.

A microscopic fungus, invisible to the naked eye.

and brown as the grass in February, but let the first raindrops fall and this "dead" moss greens up within minutes. This small, strange world is a good place to use a hand lens or a microscope. The closer we can see this miniature forest the more we can begin to understand and appreciate it.

MUSHROOMS

Mushrooms are included under the larger term *fungi*. This somewhat general term covers the vast majority of nonflowering plants, which though mostly a spring phenomenon, can be found at other times of year. Fine, threadlike hyphae form the vegetative body of these plants, similar in function and physical appearance to roots. In a mass, these hyphae are called mycelium and are the matted, white tangle we sometimes find under rotting tree bark or just under a layer of leaf mold in the woods. In some parasitic types of fungi, this reaching, thready mass actually invades

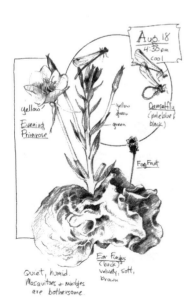

Aug. 18
4:30 pm
cool

yellow
Evening
Primrose

yellow
green
green

Damselfly
(pale blue &
black)

Fog Fruit

Ear Fungus
(back)
velvety, soft,
brown

Quiet, humid.
Mosquitoes + midges
are bothersome.

Field journal page. Ear fungus and "friends."

the host plant and may injure or kill it. The saprophytic forms exist on dead and decaying matter only, and some fungi actually form symbiotic relationships with their hosts.

The fruiting bodies of fungi take on a fantastic variety of shapes and sizes, from slime molds and algal fungi to cup and carbon fungi, as well as the more familiar and visible forms of the edible and nonedible mushrooms.

The more common types of mushrooms (those most likely to be found in your park or backyard) include gilled, pored, sac, puffball, coral, and shelf fungi. The terms are fairly descriptive of their types, but within these loose groups are a wide variety. Gilled mushrooms are perhaps the most easily recognized. The white button mushrooms available in any supermarket are of this type. Look under the cap; numerous fine divisions like the gills of a fish give this mushroom its name. Don't make the mistake of thinking that all gilled mushrooms are as edible as these, though: The deadly amanita, a close relative, is also white, gilled, and as innocent looking as a baby. Be *sure* that you have correctly identified any mushroom you find in the field before eating it. A good field guide with clear color photos or the advice of an experienced mycologist is a must. Though I eat and enjoy many varieties of wild mushrooms, this is one case where an ounce of prevention is worth a pound of cure. Eat only young, fresh mushrooms that you are quite sure of. Many mushroom varieties that will fell a strong person seem to be eaten with impunity by wildlife, so *don't* assume that a mushroom is edible simply because a squirrel or bug has nibbled it.

Field journal page. The shelf fungus (bottom of page) *had so invaded the host tree that wood pulled away with it.*

Be sure, also, that your finds are at the correct stage to eat. Many common puffballs of the order Lycoperdales are edible and delicious when young. Cut them in half to make sure the flesh is still firm and white and that they have not yet begun to dry into the powdery cloud of spores they release when fully ripe. Those clouds of tan or olive spores give this mushroom its name.

Pore mushrooms of the order Aphyllophorales have tiny, porelike tubes under their caps instead of gills. They can be both edible and poisonous. Even among the widely eaten boletes there lurks the lurid boleta (*Boletus luridas*), easily identified by the bright red or maroon pore surface. The yellow inner flesh turns blue when you cut into it. If you bring home a mushroom that has red or red-tinged pores and does this particular magic trick, throw it out or use it only for study.

The delicately flavored morels, or Morchella family, are of the sac fungus type, having neither pores nor gills but a convoluted, spongelike cap and a hollow stem. Don't confuse them with the poisonous and sometimes lethal brain gyromitra (*Gyromitra esculenta*), one of the false morels. The *Morchella esculenta* (and other closely related morels), on the other hand, is some of the finest eating this side of heaven.

Truffles (Order Tuberales), too, are sac fungi. Unless you have a specially trained dog or pig to sniff them out, you will probably not find them in your park or backyard. They grow underground, in a symbiotic relationship with tree roots.

Most shelf fungi are also pore fungi, although some such as the *Oak daedalea* have elongated, labyrinthine pores that closely resemble gills. A few have actual gills, like *Panus conchatus* and *Crepdotus mollis* of the edible shelf fungi and the dry, inedible *Schizophyllum commune*. Only a few of the shelf fungi are edible; in general they are too woody to be palatable or have a disagreeable flavor.

One notable exception is the *Polyporus sulphureus,* or chicken-of-the-woods. The pores are a sulfurous yellow that doesn't change if bruised. Spores are white, and the cap is red or orange. They often grow in a close series, looking for all the world like the ruffles on a cancan dancer's skirt. Mycelium may invade a living tree, where it can grow for many years before fruiting; then, each year, the fungus will appear at the same location.

Look for rusty-hoof fomes (*Fomes fomentarius*), which are hard, dry growths on tree bark that really do resemble the hooves of horses. They are so woody that they once were used as tinder to start fires. Artist's fungus is another common shelf type, with pure white pores that turn dark when bruised. Artists through the centuries have used this natural canvas for their drawings.

Polyporus shelves may be beautifully striated and colored. Their pore layer is difficult to separate from their woody caps. The fruiting bodies of these shelves may appear year after year at the same place. The mycelium

Rusty-hoof fomes.

often invades the heartwood of living trees, turning it into a charcoallike dark brown substance. Shelf fungi found on trees rather than on fallen logs are parasitic.

You may come across a wood ear or a tree ear on your walks. These do uncannily resemble a human ear and are soft and gelatinous to the touch. There may be only one or a whole colony growing from a dead log. *Auricularia auricula* is considered edible, but more for the texture than the flavor. A similar species, *Auricularia polytricha*, is grown as a food crop in the Orient.

Mushrooms require moisture and nutrients in the form of dead or dying organic matter. Although they perform no photosynthesis themselves, still they feed on the by-products of that process somewhere down the line.

Small, jellylike ear fungus on a field journal page showing its general ecosystem at a nearby state park.

Damp woods are a favorite habitat, but you may find them in the park, your flower garden, in an old shed (or on it, if the wood is old and rotten), or even under your house. The study of these wonderfully diverse plants can become a lifelong hobby for an amateur mycologist. Dry mushrooms for future study, or plant them in your backyard garden. A camping trip might be a good time to find many varieties and identify or study them in their natural habitat. Use your field journal for quick sketches if you don't want to disturb them.

Make a spore print, just for fun. Put the cap of your found treasure on a piece of paper overnight. Cover it with an inverted bowl so it will not be disturbed. In the morning you should have a perfect print. (If you are not sure whether this particular specimen has light or dark spores, use half-light and half-dark paper under it. This way *something* should be visible by morning.)

We have found many uses for the fungi we share our space with. Besides the edible mushrooms, fungi (yeasts) are used in the fermentation of beer, wine, and alcohol and to make bread rise. Antibiotics, enzymes, vitamins, and other helpful tricks in your doctor's little black bag are manufactured from these ancient life forms.

With few possible exceptions, no other form in nature has carried so many legends and tales. Perhaps because it does grow in darkness and doesn't flower, the mushroom (or "Toadstool" as poisonous varieties are sometimes called) has had some fantastic properties for good or evil attributed to it. Witches were said to include them in their brew. American Indians still use a relatively rare variety (*Psilocybin*) in sacred rituals when on a vision quest. (In the late 1960s and early 1970s other people experimented with these too.) Mushrooms cure and kill and provide a place for magic, as well as giving pleasure to the epicure and the amateur naturalist. What more could any plant do?

To encourage mushrooms in your own backyard, shake the paper on which you made your spore print out the back door. I often carry young edible puffballs or earthstars home. I simply "poof" advanced specimens out by the back fence, where the habitat is closest to the woods where I found them.

LICHENS

Lichens are at least as mysterious as the larger and more noticeable mushrooms, but because they exist unobtrusively on the very rocks or soil under our feet, we seldom pay them the least bit of attention. Only when huge boulders glow with an unearthly orange or pale mint green do we wonder, what's that? and go to investigate. Even the smallest rocks and twigs may harbor their cargo of lichen. Use your hand lens to get a closer look.

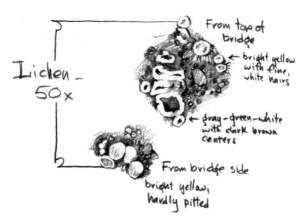

Liichen -
50x

From top of
bridge
← bright yellow
with fine,
white hairs

← gray-green-white
with dark brown
centers

From bridge side
bright yellow,
hardly pitted

*Lichen found on an
old concrete bridge.*

For years, scientists didn't understand the makeup of this humble, slow-growing plant, although they correctly classified it as a thallophyte. Before the turn of the century, Beatrix Potter, creator of Peter Rabbit (and dedicated amateur scientist), speculated that lichen was a combination of algae and fungi. Because she was young, because she was a woman, and because she illustrated charming little watercolors for children, she was simply ignored, if not laughed at. Now we know that lichen is precisely that: plump, pealike algal cells in the medulla surrounded by the tangled net of fungal hyphae in the cortex, which protects the algae and prevents its drying out. The algae produce carbohydrates that the fungus uses for food: a perfect example of a symbiotic relationship. The fungi in lichens produces spores that must be disseminated together with compatible algae in order to form other lichens. All systems must be "go" more often than not for lichens are found from the shivering tundra of the arctic circle to African rocks too hot to touch. With up to four different methods of sexual reproduction in some species the survival rate of this hardy plant is very high.

We tend to think of lichen (if we think of it at all) as tiny gray-green crusts on old bridges or rocks; but look around you. There is a vast variety of form and color here. Some lichens are black and dusty looking. Some are bright orange or yellow. Some are acid green, and some a pale, powdery mint. They may be a tightly attached, crustlike formation (crustose), loose, lettucelike shield formations on trees and logs (foliose), or perhaps stalked or shrubby (fruticose) like the red-topped British soldiers (*Cladonia cristatella*) or the branched reindeer mass (*Cladina subtenuis*).

Like mushrooms, these, too, are useful nonflowering plants. The subtle color of your Harris tweeds comes from a lichen dye. Reindeer subsist largely on the lichen form bearing their name. Physicians have made use of its curative properties. Sachets and scents were made from the powdered plants or their extracted oil, and some of our "deepest" fragrances at the perfume counter are still made up of this natural product. Arctic explorers have been saved from starvation by eating these somewhat off-

Mealy
Goblet
Lichen

Sheild lichen
on cedar

*Two kinds of lichen growing in a
Missouri Ozark park.*

putting little plants. Litmus paper, used in chemical tests for acids and
alkalis, is made with lichen.

Once you begin to look for lichen, you find it everywhere. Redeye lichen grows on rock or bark. Lollipop lichen turns the ground powdery,
and then, before disappearing, sends up tiny stalks with round, black,
disk-shaped "lollipops." Look for pink earth lichen on sterile soil, perhaps
in a ditch. Golden lichen, horsehair lichen, and beard lichen are all delicate, branched or hairlike, as far from out imaginary tight gray-green crust
as you could get.

I found this pale shield lichen growing on a cedar tree in a wonderful
park in the Missouri Ozarks. Pyxie cup (or goblet lichen) grew nearby from
a piece of rotting wood.

We know relatively little of the origin or age of lichens, since they do
not fossilize, which provides the commonest way to date life forms. They
may have evolved fairly recently, from the fungus group Ascomycetes.
Algae are ancient life forms, but the relationship of the two to become
lichen must have occurred somewhat later than the appearance of the first
algal form.

These enduring little plants are fun to grow at home. They are hardy
and beautiful year round and require very little care.

THE MOSSY PLACES

Mosses are embryophytes, or plants that form embryos at some point
in their reproductive process; a characteric they share with such diverse
species as liverworts, ferns, and conifers. These simpler forms, the bry-
ophytes, grow in moist places: on rocks, in soil, or even on the trunks of
trees. Like ferns, fungi, and horsetail (equisetum), mosses produce spores
in tiny capsules. When a spore lands on a likely spot with sufficient moisture, a green, hyphaelike thread (the protonema) grows out, takes root,

spore
capsules

lichen

Moss
with
Sheild
Lichen

Moss in association with shield lichen.

and then branches into a seaweedlike form. When buds and leafy branches form, the familiar mossy shape develops.

These are incredibly hardy plants, able to survive many successive dryings and floodings. They grow over a great part of our world, and also have proven to be useful. As mosses decay, if they are sufficient in number and conditions are favorable, they form peat, a major source of fuel in parts of the world. Peat bogs in Ireland have warmed generations of people. Peat is often mixed with garden soil to loosen and aerate it. Some houseplants grow happily in sphagnum moss with no soil at all. (Sphagnum is one of the few mosses that can be positively identified without characteristic spore cases.)

Some common mosses may be found on the walls or stones of your own backyard. Burned ground moss will even grow where soil is hard and dry. Good soil is not a requirement for a beautiful stand of mosses; they often grow on poor or acidic soil.

Your pocket microscope or a hand lens will help you identify the mosses you find. The leafy branches may look quite similar, but the spore cases will tell the story. Broom moss, (*Dicranum spp.*) apple moss, Indian brave moss, and twisted moss (*Tortella humilis*) all look very similar until you look closely. The wonderful variety in nature, even on such a tiny, intimate scale, will amaze you—and perhaps awe you as well.

You can encourage these velvet miniatures in your own backyard with sufficient moisture and a friendly, acidic pH. Keep patio stones or your rock garden well watered. If you bring in moss from the wild, first roughen the soil and then wet it down well. Tamp the moss firmly into place so there are no air pockets underneath or it will dry out. Keep it moist until it "takes." A friend suggests mixing a bit of buttermilk with water to encourage mossy growth.

Try a terrarium. An old fish tank, a large glass jar, or even a brandy snifter will do well. Put in a bit of garden soil, well tamped and watered, and add your mosses; use as many different kinds as you can find. Add lichen, if you like. Another friend often adds scarlet cup mushrooms and the beautiful earthstars to her terrarium. Keep it damp and out of direct sun and it will last for years. You can try covering it with a piece of glass, but be sure to let it get a bit of fresh air each day.

Mosses, lichens, and mushrooms are not the only nonflowering plants. Algae and diatoms are considered the simplest forms. Stoneworts, liverworts, horsetails, and ferns are higher on the family tree. Plant evolution has produced successively larger and more complex forms, but they all have a link to the far-distant past that perhaps lends them an air of mystery.

TEN

Canada geese before migration.

Birds: A Personal Study

Birds are among the first things we notice when we turn our infant attention outside the safe circle of mother, father, and the four walls of our own safe nest. Moving shapes, bright colors, beautiful sounds—we are immediately alert to this new creature in our sensory awareness.

If we are fortunate indeed, that childlike wonder may last a lifetime; there are certainly birds in plenty to warrant our interest. At first the common feeder birds may be enough—the cardinals and chickadees and even the sparrows. As our interest expands, it grows to include the more exotic birds, the ones which seldom (or never) visit a feeder in normal times. We learn the names, the songs, the field marks of rails and gallinules, herons and accipiters. The private lives of birds can become a lifelong study.

Their evolution as well as the dizzying variety of their mating and nesting habits fascinate us, and if we are honest, we'll admit—we envy them. If we could only fly!

DINOSAUR BIRDS

Are birds really the last of the dinosaurs, somehow having escaped extinction by an eleventh-hour adaptation in the form of hollow bones and feathers? It's hard to believe when looking at the prettily patterned song-bird, pert and tiny, at the backyard feeder, but easier to discern in the bigger birds—egrets, cormorants, grebes. Something in those strange, scaly feet and beadlike eyes may give away the family resemblance.

BIRD STUDIES

Bird books often cover the activities of the more popular species: the songbirds; the birds at your backyard feeder. If they do not, we often seem to concentrate our attention here, on the birds we consider pretty or pert. Consider the life and times of some of the more unusual birds: herons, cormorants, killdeer, hawks, eagles, ospreys, shorebirds, and wad-ers or less popular birds like jays, crows, and starlings, which are often called trash birds.

Get to know the birds by observation, attracting them if you can. Per-haps birds are popular subject of study because they are almost always *there,* so dependably available in one form or another except on the hot-test, stillest afternoons—and even then we can see them high in the sky like grains of pepper.

Use owl-call tapes at any time of the year to attract small perching birds, or try the "pssht-pssht" call. No one seems to know why this particular sound attracts birds. Perhaps it is similar to a feeding or scolding sound. At any rate, it seems to arouse the birds' curiosity.

In his delightful book* Joseph Cornell offers a number of suggestions for attracting birds close enough really to *see* them. My favorite is called "birds on a stick." The watcher sits quietly, perhaps camouflaged with a blanket or a poncho, eyes hidden by the blanket or by a large hat. He or she holds a long, branched stick and utters the "pssht-pssht" call (Cornell opts for a "phssh-phssh" variation). If the watcher is very lucky, the birds may land on the stick. A Carolina wren inspected me closely as I tried this trick.

A variation of this camouflage may attract your backyard feeder birds to eat from your hand. Near your feeder, put out a scarecrow with an outstretched "hand." An old glove or a tin pie plate forms the feeding platform. Fill this auxiliary feeder with goodies, and let your birds get used to it. Then borrow the scarecrow's wardrobe and pan and stand as close as possible to the normal feeding spot, arm outstretched. Hold very still and you may feel a bit like Saint Francis when the birds settle happily to feast at your outstretched hand.

---

*Cornell, Joseph Bharat, *Sharing Nature with Children.* Calif.: Ananda Publications, 1979.

BIRD MIGRATIONS

The great seasonal movements of millions of birds north to their summer breeding grounds and then south again for the winter provide us with some of the finest opportunities we may have for seeing some of the less common species. As they pass through, we may hear a musical series of notes we have heard at no other time. Who was that stranger that paused for a day or two and then moved on with the warming air? Great flocks of songbirds pass through, and those who find our area to be home will settle down and let the rest pass.

Hawk migrations are exciting more interest each year as the gliding predators travel in huge "kettles," floating together in the drifting air currents. In some places these migratory paths are well mapped, and hundreds of people line the ridges where they pass. According to the Audubon Society's Field Guide* over nineteen thousand hawks, mainly broad wings, were observed as they passed the lookout at Hawk Mountain, Pennsylvania, on a single day. This is the best time to observe the normally secretive broad wings. They live in the forest canopy and may only advertise their presence by a thin, uncharacteristic "keeee."

Canada geese are known to fly over three hundred miles in a night (quite a feat when you consider they may migrate through some of the worst flying weather of the year). Long-lived birds, in captivity they may reach ages up to seventy years. (In the wild, a lifespan of seven to ten years is more common as habitats shrink and more birds are poisoned with lead shot; many of the birds that hunters don't kill outright fall ill from high levels of lead in their bloodstreams.) These great, honking birds are monogamous, and they mate for life.

Redwing blackbirds migrate in large groups. No change of season is complete for me without sighting at least one bare tree, fully "leafed" with blackbirds showing off their scarlet epaulets and voicing their communal cacophony.

BIRD NEIGHBORS

Even birds I have known all my life can still surprise me with some new variation on their avian theme. Titmice mating with cheerful abandon in the early winter; a late-November bluebird like a dream of summer; a flock of a hundred robins hurrying south on Thanksgiving day, and running late, by the look of it—I never know what to expect, even from these old familiar friends. My new attention rewards me with fresh delights almost every day.

Audubon Society Field Guide to North American Birds. New York: Alfred A. Knopf, 1977.

Even the most common feeder birds can surprise us if we watch.

Listen for the blue jays in your own backyard; their "tool-ools," "keuues," and "wheedledees" will amaze you if you expected only a raucous "jay, jay!" A starling in winter's iridescent dotted swiss garb carries on a front-yard jam session in a staggering variety of toots and whistles—it's as if an old friend suddenly spoke in twenty different languages. And watch your feeder closely, especially after an ice storm or a heavy snow—you may play host to visitors you never expected. The "new kid on the block" can provide you with sleuthing opportunities as you search for clues to his identity as well as offering hours of sheer pleasure just in the watching.

THE PREDATORS

I love the small singing birds of the park and backyard, but even more I love the beautiful, sinewy predators. The deadly accuracy of a hawk's plunge—perhaps from hundreds of feet—to capture the prey never fails to excite my admiration. If we can watch their hunt dispassionately, we can't help but admire the grace and purpose of the falcons, ospreys, ea-

These owls are still common in my area; even the increasingly rare barn owl is sighted on occasion.

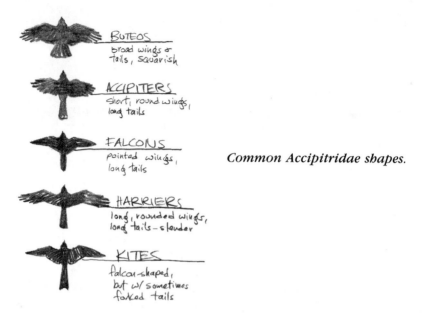

BUTEOS
broad wings &
tails, squarish

ACCIPITERS
short, round wings,
long tails

FALCONS
pointed wings,
long tails

Common Accipitridae shapes.

HARRIERS
long, rounded wings,
long tails - slender

KITES
falcon-shaped,
but w/ sometimes
forked tails

gles, and other members of the Accipitridae family, or the wonderful ef-
ficiency of the owl clan, members of the families Tytonidae (barn owls)
and Strigidae. There is nothing more beautiful than the way the Accipitridae hawks (subfamilies include accipiters, harriers, buteos, and falcons)
hover in the air as if it were a solid, lifting hand, making flight look as
effortless as lying in bed on a cold winter morning.

Learn to identify these birds by their flight patterns and overall shapes.
Red-tailed hawks and other buteos (or buzzard hawks) are compact, almost chubby, with broad wings and rounded tails. You can see them soaring, wheeling slowly in the dome of the sky. If you are close enough you
can see them turn their heads to search for the movement of prey. The
eagles and ospreys are immense, even from the ground. The golden eagle
we saw at the state park had a wingspan of close to eight feet; the osprey
at Rocky Hollow had a six-foot reach. Look for the osprey's characteristic
black wrists against the light underwings. This bird holds it wings kinked
and its tail fanned in flight. You'll know you've seen an osprey if the bird
dives feet first for fish. According to Peterson, you may see one anywhere
except Antarctica, a wide-enough range for any bird.

The bald eagle's wings are held flat; compare that to the turkey vulture's
dihedral angle. The harriers (or marsh hawks) carry their wings in low,
gliding flight in a similar angle to the turkey vulture's, and their tails are
long and slender. The accipiters (or bird hawks) are like flying T's with a
heavy, rounded crossbar. Their bodies and tails seem stretched long in
comparison to their short wings. These birds fly with several beats and
then a short glide. Cooper's hawks, goshawks, and sharp-shinned hawks
are among this subfamily.

Red-tailed hawk.

If you see a hawk with powerful, pointed wings and a long tail, chances are you've spotted a falcon. The American kestrel (or sparrow hawk) is a tiny, colorful member of this clan. Only as big as a good-sized robin, it's unmistakably a predator, with its hooked beak and curved talons.

These daytime predators have different facial structure than owls. Where the night hunters have rounded, front-facing eyes, the eyes of hawks and eagles are placed on either side of the skull to allow a broad range of vision while hunting, and are hooded to shield them from the sun.

If you live in the South, watch for kites overhead, the graceful birds of prey with pointed wings. The swallow-tailed kite has an unmistakable forked tail. The Mississippi kite, a beautiful gray-and-white bird, is seen near the rivers, streams, or shelterbelts. These birds are normally southerners, but their range is rapidly spreading northward.

THE WATER BIRDS

Here I don't mean specifically those birds called waterfowl—the ducks and geese common to our ponds, lakes, and waterways—but a broader category that includes the herons, cormorants, grebes, and shorebirds, including killdeer. Although you'll see these last near almost any body of water you may have in your park or backyard, you'll also find them in open farmland, running down a country lane like a cartoon roadrunner, and keening plaintively over any shopping-center parking lot. They range from Canada to Mexico and coastal Peru, so wherever you are you're not

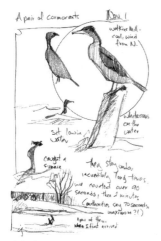

Field journal page. Cormorants.

likely to miss that loud "kill-dee, kill-de-ah!" Their dapper black double bib distinguishes them from others of the belted plover clan, and the flash of a tawny rump in flight confirms identification.

If your park has a pond you may be lucky enough to watch herons and cormorants busy with their lives and interacting with other water-loving species. The storklike legs of the tall herons seem to bend backward at the knee—and so they do. It's fun to watch them stepping carefully on those long legs and wading stealthily into the shallow water where they fish. They are extremely efficient hunters. You may very well see one spear prey with that long beak.

Cormorants eat small fish and crustaceans. They sometimes perform a characteristic fishing feat of cooperation, making a fan-shaped formation with their bodies together, and driving their prey before them until concentrated enough for easy fishing. Unlike most water birds, cormorants don't have abundant oil glands that would keep their feathers waterproof. It is this—and a singular ability to compress the air from their bodies—that allows them to dive from five to twenty-five feet under the water's surface after prey. When you see them, wings spread wide in the sun, they have hung themselves out to dry.

Watch closely where you live. Take your binoculars or telescope to your local park. You may have the opportunity to see an entire tree decorated with great egrets, cattle egrets, and snowy egrets, as if a band of angels had chosen one dead tree for their epiphany.

PROVIDING HABITAT AT HOME

This may be as simple as allowing a corner of your yard to "go wild," but you may want to carry it a step or two further to offer your birds what they particularly like. As in chapter one, we can make a special place for birds by what we choose to plant (sunflowers, old-man's beard) and by which wildings we encourage. Dock is a popular seed plant, as is the hay fever sufferer's nemesis, ragweed. I see my backyard birds enjoying the mealy seeds of lamb's-quarters as well as seeds from the various wild sunflower family members. These are known to feed over fifty species of wild birds and are beautiful enough to deserve a place in any garden. Gayfeather and other members of the *Liatris* clan are favorite seed-bearing wild flowers. Zinnias, asters, and daisies, if left standing into the fall and winter, are also popular. Bushes, vines, or trees that have berries of almost any sort are good bird feeders. Consider planting hawthorn, serviceberry, dogwood, honeysuckle, hackberry, or linden in your yard. Many birds favor the small, tart crab apples; you might also attract deer if you are near a wooded area.

Check with your local chapter of the Audubon Society to see what "bird plants" grow well in your particular area, and don't be too quick to weed your garden.

A source of running water attracts a great many birds that might not look twice at a birdbath full of stale water. A small recirculating pump can provide both you and your avian visitors with hours of pleasure.

FEEDERS AND NESTS. Part of providing habitat, of course, is encouraging birds to nest near your house and seeing to their needs in the winter. You may attract an interesting summer crowd with a variety of nest boxes. Special styles and entrance holes can attract a wide range of birds while discouraging other, less desired species (starlings, cowbirds, pigeons).

Remember, your backyard habitat changes from year to year. Trees or bushes die out or grow large. Areas that were formerly garden are now wild. These changes in your minihabitat should be taken into consideration when placing nest boxes. Some birds like to nest near (or in) buildings, while others will want to be as far from you as they can get. Some

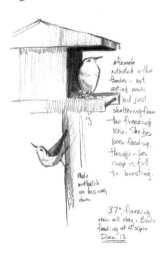

Nuthatches at the feeder.

like cover, and others prefer open spaces. As your yard changes with the years, try moving your birdhouses to different spots. If you haven't had a family of wrens for several years, move the birdhouse; you may just hit on the perfect spot. The birds know what they prefer, so try different areas or types of habitat until one shows an interest in your proffered housing.

Wren houses must be constructed with tiny holes just large enough for their intended occupants (one inch for house and Bewick's wrens, one-and-one-eighth inch for Carolina wrens).

Put up bluebird houses as far from your home and outbuildings as possible. Competition from sparrows near your dwelling is too fierce for bluebird nesting. Perhaps you may even get permission to put up these boxes in your park. (Check with your city's parks and recreation department.)

If you have a pond on your property, you might want to sink a post in the water and attach an old tin washtub just above the water's surface. You might encourage a family of geese, if they feel they have a safe, predator-resistant place to raise their young.

If you have dead trees on your acreage (even if the "acreage" is only a small lot in town as ours is) don't be too quick to cut them down. If they don't threaten the house or passersby, they are wonderful as homes for everything from woodpeckers and flickers to bluebirds and screech owls (and even a squirrel or a raccoon or two). If your woodpeckers are not drilling nest holes quickly enough, a large bit for your electric or hand drill can remedy the situation. Many small birds will take advantage of your good beginning and excavate a suitable nest to fit their own tastes in construction.

I like to offer a wide variety of feeders to attract as many kinds of birds as possible and to keep them from starving in extremely harsh weather. A suet/seed feeder is for protein. A vertical finch feeder attracts the goldfinches, buntings, siskins, and a few chickadees and juncos. A large covered platform is for everybody. Those birds that don't like to eat from a platform enjoy the feast spilled on the ground below. Although wrens don't normally frequent feeders, you may see one furtively check out your platform feeder just before flying away.

Nothing need go to waste. Birds will enjoy leftover cereal and vegetables, buggy grain, meat scraps, bacon grease, or shortening; use your imagination. Some birds even favor boiled or mashed potatoes. Birds seem especially fond of white bread. Use it to attract them rather than to provide their staple diet, though—it is often not so nutritionally complete as other grains and seeds. Winter wrens and Bewick's wrens may be attracted to bits of raw hamburger or ground nut meats.

Those sometimes troublesome imports from Europe, the starlings, are not really picky eaters. They don't care for sunflowers in the shell, buckwheat, or thistle, but they will take a wide variety of grains as well as some oddities (American cheese, grapefruit, eggs, sauerkraut).

*Field journal page.
Bird-banding
demonstration.*

Our local nature sanctuary offers classes in building bird feeders from found objects like pie plates, trays, and cookie sheets. You needn't spend a fortune on feeders or feed.

BIRD BANDING

To get to know the birds "up close and personal," attend a bird-banding demonstration or learn to do it yourself and get a license. The nature sanctuary in Liberty offers such demonstrations, and so I was able to hold a variety of small backyard birds in my hands. I will never feel the same about a chickadee or junco now that I've felt the tiny heart beating rapidly in my hand. I was allowed to hold them to draw; it was a privilege that quite humbled me as I tried to calm the frightened little birds. We were taught how to look for fat deposits (to see how well the birds were faring in the winter weather) by blowing aside the breast feathers to see the translucent skin. Go to a demonstration, if you get the chance.

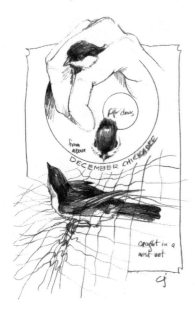

Field journal page. Chickadees in a mist net.

LOST AND INJURED BIRDS

If you find a fledgling fallen from the nest, it is best *not* to try to "rescue" it—at least not to try to raise it. It is a tremendous and often heartbreaking responsibility. If the bird is too young, it will probably die anyway. You will have to feed it often throughout the night, every four hours or even more frequently. You'll need to identify its species, which is often more difficult than you'd imagine from this gangly, naked, big-beaked little creature unless its parents are nearby. Identify it you must if you are planning to feed it; otherwise you won't know what it needs.

The best course of action is to look for the parents and the nest. If you can find it, replace the bird as soon as possible—some injured birds may simply need a bit of rest. If not, put it as high as you can reach in the safety of a bush or a small tree; the parents will continue to feed it there. If you have no other choice and must attempt to save the fledgling yourself, handle it as little and as gently as possible and check with your veterinarian or local conservation commission officer for help. (It is illegal to have some wild birds in your possession—again, call your conservation officer.)

squirrel with
hedge apple

*Curious fox squirrels in
the park: They often
stop to watch us.*

Park and Backyard Mammals

We share a special kinship with other mammals, a bond of like for like. We, too, are warm-blooded creatures. We, too, feed our helpless young from our own bodies. These mammals are as aware of our presence as we are of theirs. Once we've spotted one of them, we can't help but watch a wild thing until it chooses to break the spell by bolting. Perhaps that's why, when we encounter some mammal in the woods, we feel a sudden thrill—even if it is only a scolding fox squirrel or a chipmunk.

Because these creatures are so aware, they are also wary. Birds generally go on about their business, ignoring us entirely unless we get too close. Some mammals, on the other hand, "watch us like a hawk." They usually know we are there as soon as we enter their territory, and they may continue to watch us until we are forced by our screaming muscles to move.

It is as if they are as curious about us as we are them. Have you ever spotted a deer in the woods? Instead of bounding instantly away, it often hesitates, big ears swiveling, eyes boring into ours until we are both nearly hypnotized. In our park, I held the attention of a mother deer and her almost fully grown fawns by making silly noises at them: a series of loud smacks and kisses and whistles. They did move away (no doubt from someone they considered a bit crazy), but slowly, looking back often and stopping to watch me.

103

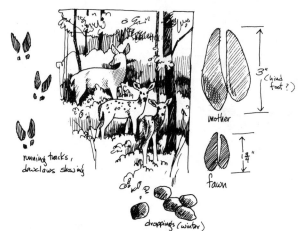

running tracks,
dewclaws showing

3" (hind foot?)

mother

fawn

1¾"

droppings (winter)

*A doe and her fawns;
the mother is wary,
but the young as
curious as any young
thing.*

We can develop skills that will allow us to get close enough to observe animals going about their business of feeding and mating and caring for their young. As mentioned in chapters two and three, we can learn stalking skills. Sometimes simply being preoccupied with our field notes or sketches will be sufficient to reassure an animal that we mean no harm, especially if we are seated. One day as I silently sketched the "widow-maker" chewed by beavers I was lucky enough to see a muskrat, as near to me as one of my cats would come, having a bit of lunch at the edge of the stream.

You may see most wildlife from the relative anonymity of your car; often, they choose to use the same cleared roadway that we do. The number of road kills attests to that, unfortunately. By driving carefully in the

*Field journal page. I wonder if the beaver
who tried to cut down this
"widowmaker" was injured by the split?*

park or countryside, taking it slow and easy, we may have the chance to see many wild animals, perhaps on their way to a feast. Even in the daytime we've seen particularly active raccoons and opossums near a ripe field of corn. Apparently the proximity of such plenty overcame their normal nocturnal caution.

ROAD AND PREDATOR KILLS

Unfortunately, most often the amateur naturalist gets the chance to study closely an animal's physical structure when it's dead. Overcoming our natural aversion to death is a must; I put myself into a "scientific" mode, becoming as dispassionate as possible, when I come across an animal that is beyond help. Now I can see how the fur grows, changing direction at the bridge of the nose, along the neck, or at the elbows. I can study the kind of feet and toes that have evolved for this animal's particular needs: the river otter's webbed toes, so well suited for cutting through the water, or the squirrel's delicately articulated "hands."

Occasionally a cat or some other predator will leave a backyard kill apparently undamaged, or perhaps an animal has simply died of natural causes. At any rate, we can take this opportunity to get to know these creatures intimately. Sketch them quickly, if you can, from several angles; take measurements. Do a close-up of paws or tails or head details. Take photos, if you don't sketch; and make notes. You may be able to determine such things as whether the animal is young or old, or well fed or verging on starvation, and you may make some educated guesses as to habitat conditions.

If it is summer, you will only want to sketch fresh kills. The smell and the flies make such an activity impossible for all but the most stouthearted. It is best not to touch the animal. They are almost always covered with

I had the chance to draw this fox squirrel on a chilly November day.

fleas and lice, which sense the loss of their warm-blooded habitat almost immediately and go searching for a new home. Don't let it be you. If you need to move the animal for a better view, use a stick. It is always possible that the animal you find has died of rabies. You can't catch this disease by merely touching the fur, but you can cut yourself on the teeth or get the animal's saliva into a fresh scratch. This is a case when it is better to be safe than sorry.

When you are finished, you can move it to a ditch or the woods, where it will provide a welcome meal for scavengers. Crows or vultures will find it, or hawks, owls, or coyotes may get badly needed nourishment if hunting has been bad.

INJURED AND "ABANDONED" ANIMALS

A mammal with a minor injury is much like a fledgling bird fallen from the nest. Often our misguided attempts to help put the creature under more stress than we are able to counteract. If you find such an animal, handle it as little as possible (if at all; it may have a disease that could be transmitted to your household pets, or it may be frightened and angry enough to put up quite a fight, causing you to get bitten or scratched). Confine it, if possible, in a humane cage, and call your local office of the state conservation commission or your veterinarian for advice. They will know what treatment to recommend, if any. Most often, however, they will simply suggest that the animal be destroyed. It is against the law to have a feral fur-bearing animal in your possession in most areas. Your conservation commission will be able to tell you if you are breaking the law and will usually arrange to pick up the injured animal.

If you uncover a nest of young rabbits with your lawn mower or find a litter of tiny, hairless squirrels in a hollow tree, don't assume they need help or that their mother has abandoned them. A mother rabbit nurses her babies in the early morning and late afternoon. The rest of the time she stays away, wisely knowing that her presence will attract the attention of predators to her helpless family. Many very young animals are nearly scentless. They will not be harmed if we leave them be.

Unless you know the mother has been killed and will not return, it is usually best to do nothing. A young fawn can lie undetected in the grass with a fox or your family dog sniffing only inches away.

PREDATOR AND PREY

Words are powerful psychological triggers, and few trigger more emotional reactions than these. The word *predator* evokes frightening images of violence and blood and death, of the strong and ruthless conquering the weak and helpless—the *preyed upon*. Even the dictionary defines *predatory* as "addicted to or living by plunder, pillage, robbery or exploitation; habitually preying on other animals." It sounds like a fatal character flaw, a perverse choice of evil over good; as if the animal in question could *decide* to eat grass, fruits, and grain henceforth and forevermore.

Simply put and with as few emotional overtones as possible, a predator is a carnivorous creature; that is, it lives by eating meat. Instinct, evolution, divine order—whatever you choose to call it, these animals are programmed to find their sustenance high up on the food chain. It is a definition many wild creatures share with humans, but in our increasingly unnatural society, the role of predator is "officially" taken only by a select few and the rest of us purchase our meat neatly wrapped, sanitized, and de-emotionalized in the well-lighted and clean environment of the local supermarket. Only the hunters and farmers among us still experience firsthand what it means to be a predator, a flesh-eating creature, killing its own meat. When we come down to it, though, we are all akin to the wolf, the bear, the barn owl, and the hawk. The predators in the park are not so very different from us.

It is hard to learn to be dispassionate about the predator/prey relationship, but as we spend more time outdoors we are able to accept the death of a young rabbit as it feeds and nourishes a mother fox and her kits. Another day, the rabbit's uncanny ability to change direction in midstream may let it go free.

When the predator/prey relationship is in balance, generally only the old, weak, or very young animals are taken. Since timber wolves have been extirpated from the boundaries of Yellowstone Park (only a few natural packs still exist in the northern part of the contiguous United States), deer populations have exploded. Where before the sight of a thin, sickly animal was a rare exception, it threatens to become the rule as the browsing animals compete for available food supplies. As I write this, the federal government is considering a plan to reintroduce *Canis lupus* to the boundaries of the park. Surprisingly, seventy-four percent of visitors to the park said they would like to see this step taken. Prejudice in the form of unfounded fears of "the big, bad wolf" is surfacing among area farmers, however, and the battle may be a hard one to win. Everyone agrees that our national symbol, the magnificent bald eagle, should be saved from extinction. No one questions the fight to save the California condor. The wolf seems to be another story, though.

Here in Missouri, the red wolf (*Canis rufus*) may have paid for our prejudice in near extinction. It is also on federal endangered species lists. Stock owners have contributed to this loss, but hybridization of genes with the booming coyote population has also served to blur the lines between the species. The red wolf may occasionally chase deer, but its primary foods are rabbits, small rodents, and birds—not livestock.

A more common predator in our small-town parks is the coyote (*Canis latrans*), whose fur has unfortunately proven a popular substitute for mink on the backs of fashionable women. This animal, too, is a victim of unfounded prejudice. It is actually extremely intelligent and quick (cruising speed twenty-five to thirty miles per hour) and is a strong swimmer. The coyote feeds mainly on small rodents or birds. It may feed on carrion if the opportunity presents itself, or it may cleverly take advantage of a badger's prey, waiting at the opposite end of an escape tunnel for their common food.

Predator/prey relationships maintain the delicate balance of an ecosystem already overstrained by loss of habitat and overuse of herbicides and pesticides. Each animal has its advantages and disadvantages in the hunt. Don't imagine that the prey is a helpless and inevitable victim. Speed, camouflage, lack of scent, well-constructed burrows with a number of escape routes, or simply the ability to fly keeps the odds fairly even.

MAMMAL SIGNS

How can you tell that wild animals have passed through your backyard or park if you haven't seen them? Humans have been tracking animals for eons. We watch for tracks or scat (droppings) or bits of fur or hair to tell the tale. An experienced tracker can read a story in the snow—and so can you, with a bit of practice.

Get to know the tracks of mammals in your neighborhood. Those of

Field journal page. Raccoon tracks, rose hips, a tiny mushroom.

web bbed toes

Beaver Prints

(I measured on my arm, then checked at home. big claws They were 8½" long. He must be immense.)

If you don't have a ruler along, measure on your hand or arm, then measure at home. Early this summer there were beaver tracks a few blocks from home many times—I never did get to see their maker.

cats and dogs are easy to identify, but also look for the tracks of squirrels, voles, beaver, muskrats, and the small "handprints" of raccoons. A fox drags that big brush of a tail and leaves marks in the snow; dogs usually hold their tails aloft.

Fresh snow is a *tabula rasa,* a blank slate upon which the day's (or night's) activity is written clearly. You can even judge the time elapsed since the tracks were made—are they crisp and sharp? Has blowing snow begun to fill them in? Has alternate thawing and refreezing softened the contours or enlarged them out of all proportion? (Who knows, Bigfoot's track may only be a melted footprint in the snow.) The mud at creekbank or on a lakeshore is an excellent place to read signs. All animals must drink, so we find a great variety of fresh tracks at the water's edge.

Watch for scat on game trails. You can identify many animals by the size, shape, and contents of their droppings. Or look for owl or hawk pellets. These large predators often eat the whole of small prey; later they disgorge the indigestible hair and small bones. Hair or fur by the path may tell you where a mother rabbit has made a nest for her young—or lost her life. Where a pair of buck deer have fought, there may be bits of coarse, hollow hair and spots of blood.

Think like a tracker, follow signs, and use a good field guide to animal tracks. Soon you will be reading these cryptic runes with the best.

THE ADAPTERS

The animals we will most often see in our parks and backyards have learned to adapt—and adapt well—to our presence. Even in the city you may see an opossum in your compost heap or a raccoon leading her family right down the middle of a main street late one night. When we lived in

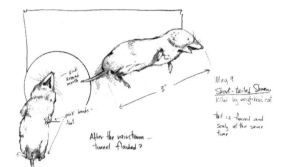

May 9
Short-tailed Shrew
Killed by neighbor's cat

tail is furred and
scaly at the same
time

After the rainstorm —
tunnel flooded ?

pink hands
tail

pink around
mouth

3"

A neighbor brought this for identification; it proved to be a short-tailed shrew.

Kansas City we occasionally caught the scent of skunk on the night air. Coyotes do well on the outskirts of towns and villages. Moles, voles, and mice go about their business, oblivious to our presence, as do the tiniest mammals of all, the shrews. Squirrels may learn to feed from our hands and certainly seem well able to survive in good numbers in our local parks.

SHREWS. These are amazingly agressive little creatures when aroused. These little eating machines are well equipped with a mouthful of sharp teeth. They are insectivorous and have a very high basal metabolism; they must eat almost constantly.

The shrew's vocabulary of clicks, twitters, and chirps varies from low-intensity sounds to a very high, ultrasonic range inaudible to our ears.

Least shrews may cooperate in tunnel building. Several may work to-gether to construct a communal burrow. Charles Schwartz* tells of two shrews in captivity that managed to make a tunnel two feet long, with four openings, in the space of two hours. That's not bad for an animal just over one-and-one-half inches long.

The short-tailed shrew killed by my neighbor's cat was a giant in com-parison: three inches long from rump to snout. Normally an underground creature, this one had ventured up after a rainstorm had flooded its bur-row.

HOUSE MICE. These are the poor little fellows that often share our homes and frighten some people (and some elephants, according to legend). A native of central Asia, they probably reached North America by way of Europe (as did many of the rats that threaten to overrun our farms, cities, and seaports). The house mouse (*Mus musculus*) lives in old fields, road-sides, old barns, and cultivated grain fields. You'll know you've found its home if you come across a nest of shredded paper, fabrics, feathers, or grass. In our old woodshed I once opened a chest of drawers to find an

---

*Schwartz, Charles, and Elizabeth R. Schwartz, *The Wild Mammals of Missouri*. University of Missouri Press and the Missouri Department of Conservation, 1981. This complete and wide-ranging guide is of special interest to midwestern naturalists.

This little fellow wandered into my house after a cold snap.

Eastern Harvest Mouse (with my ink-pen cap for scale.)

irate mother intent on protecting her litter. Comfortably ensconced in the remains of some of my old drawings, she had provided well for her young family, with a cache of grain, chicken scratch, dog food, roaches, and water bugs. I shut the drawer carefully and let her be.

HARVEST MICE. These small, shy creatures usually venture inside only when the weather turns cold. They may look for refuge in a warm crack in your foundation and then turn up, panicked and running, in your kitchen. They normally nest outdoors, storing grain and seeds nearby.

The harvest mouse's head takes up over a third of the length of its body, not including the tail. Both the eastern harvest mouse and the western harvest mouse are members of the Reithrodontomys clan.

OPOSSUMS. Opossums are curious creatures, one of the few of the order Marsupialia to inhabit North America. Most of the other species occur in Australia, including koalas, kangaroos, and wombats. The opossums scientific name is *Didelphis virginiana. Didelphis,* of Greek origin, means "double womb" and may refer to the creature's pouch, which acts as a kind of auxiliary womb where the helpless young continue to develop as if they were still inside the mother's body. The warm, fur-lined pouch contains the teats. At birth the blind, hairless youngsters make their way in a perilous journey up over the belly and into the safety of this second "womb" by instinct alone.

Look for the handlike prints of opossums in the mud. The hind foot is quite similar to the feet of primates and suits the opossum well for climbing; the thumb is almost opposite.

You have no doubt heard the expression "playing 'possum." These animals actually do play dead when frightened, a common defense that they use after baring their teeth, hissing, and dripping saliva fails.

I had the chance to get well acquainted with these fascinating mammals when a family of them took up residence in my basement one year, at-

Raccoons are endearing little beasts, even if they can be a nuisance: They seem to be able to open any garbage can made.

tracted by the warm basement and the cat's food dish. When my veterinarian told me that if I evicted the wild family at that time of year they would probably die, all the available den sites having been long since taken, we spent the winter getting to know a family of marsupials at close hand. They often hissed defensively when I opened the door, but they became as used to my presence as I was to theirs.

RACCOONS. Raccoons are among the most endearing and interesting mammals we encounter. Those bandit masks and intelligent faces—not to mention tales of the escapades of hand-raised raccoon "children"—make us perhaps more tolerant of sharing our space with them than with other wild creatures. My cousin often watched as a mother raccoon led her small family up his garden stairs at the edge of the park and onto his deck for a handout as bold as brass.

These clever animals are members of the same family as the panda of the high mountain forests of China and Tibet. The masked face is perhaps the only sign of family resemblance. In this country the other members of the clan Procyonidae are the ringtail (miner's cat or civet cat) and the coati, both of which occur only in the Far West and the Southwest.

You'll find the ubiquitous *Procyon lotor*'s (*lotor* means washer, and refers to their habit of sometimes washing their food before eating it) tracks along the banks of streams or ponds. Cornfields are a favorite habitat, too, as anyone who has tried to grow sweet corn can tell you. These tracks bear a resemblance to the footprints of a miniature human; the hind foot looks like that of a human with very long toes.

Raccoons are somewhat sedentary, with a relatively small range, but a male may travel miles to find a mate. They normally prefer dense hardwoods for a home, but they are adaptable creatures and may even occupy a niche in the inner city. They will have several dens within the range and seem to move around from one to the other as if taking time off for vacation.

Raccoons eat prodigiously during the late fall. If you see one at this time of year it will be quite a butterball, if the harvest has been good. During the winter months they may lose up to fifty percent of total body weight.

SKUNKS. Skunks are handsome animals, but not ones I'd welcome into my home as I did the opossum family. Skunks hold enough of this scent in their anal glands for five or six good sprays, but they seldom need more than the initial blast. They are able to shoot this aromatic defense up to fifteen feet, with the mist traveling perhaps three times as far; woe be to any animal—or human—that doesn't take the hint!

Skunks do give fair warning. They will snarl, hiss, stamp their front paws, and otherwise threaten mayhem. If the unlucky intruder doesn't heed the warning, the skunk turns tail—but not to run. Lifting its tail straight up, it makes a U of its body, aiming for the face, and all too often hitting it.

In our area, the striped skunk (*Mephitis mephitis*) is most common. Where you live you may see the eastern spotted (*Spilogale putorius*) or the hog-nosed skunk (*Concepatus mesoleucus*). Check with a good field guide to identify the species most likely to be in your area.

RABBITS AND HARES. Early in the morning or just as evening falls, you may spot a big-eared visitor to your park or backyard garden. The eastern cottontail is the most common member of the Leporidae clan to frequent my park. Its large, bulging eyes allow it to spot a predator in a wide range. Those huge, swiveling ears, like sonar equipment, are always on the alert. When alarmed, they utter a piercing distress cry.

Most rabbits and hares simply have forms, or shallow depressions, in the ground to serve as nests—unlike their European cousins, which excavate elaborate underground warrens. Cottontails do build nests for their undeveloped young, though. You may find a pile of soft, downy rabbit fur in a depression in the ground. Don't assume a cottontail "bit the dust" here, unless you see signs of a struggle—this may be a warm, insulated nest for immature rabbits. The mother pulls fur from her own belly to line the nest for her young.

If you have too many rabbits visiting your vegetable garden, try a bit of bone meal or blood meal around the perimeter. The scent may frighten away unwanted company.

This oak tree was split, its bark thrown hundreds of feet, and its leaves cooked to winter crispness in a single flash of lightning.

After the Storm

THUNDERSTORM

The lightning was a frightening 1812 Overture of sound and fury. When the cease fire was called, the damage was extensive—not surprising, given the power of electricity. Lightning split a giant oak tree on the hill from the highest branches to the ground, throwing the earth aside like a blanket. According to the central headquarters of the National Severe Storms Forecast Center in Kansas City, the electrical potential of a lightning flash can approach one hundred million volts. The negative and positive charges must overcome the resistance of the insulating air and find a path to the ground before a lightning bolt can form—the old oak was that path.

Floodwaters have changed the face of the land and the shape of the creek itself. Highwater debris hangs like unkempt hair from limbs now over my head. The sandbar where a muskrat made his home has been scoured away by the water. A huge dead tree floated downstream and lodged there, its branches forming an obstruction that made a powerful whirlpool in the deep, moving waters. The sandbar was carried away as if it had never been, and the muskrat's safe haven with it. Even great boulders have been lifted like freshwater mussel shells and moved downstream. The stepping stones I thought were eternal are now too far apart to traverse.

The creek itself once changed its course in some earlier, distant flood. A floating obstruction must have lodged between the banks, blocking its

The floodwater shoots up the trunk of the sycamore sapling in the creek, like an Elizabethan collar of lace.

The floodwaters erase all signs of where the banks were. Only saplings like this one tell the story.

I startled away two snakes downstream from the sapling; I made the mistake of addressing them in English! They disappeared under the muddy water.

familiar bed, and suddenly, overnight, the creek moved two hundred yards to the south, biting through to rocks buried since the last glacier receded from this corner of Missouri. A small oxbow slough now marks the former bed, a microcosm of the oxbow lakes you may find near any big river.

Even small changes after a storm are fun to note in my field journal. Which trees have lost the most twigs, leaves, or even whole limbs? The hardwood walnuts seem most susceptible to damage—even more so than the oaks. They break rather than bending like the flexible willows.

The debris at the edge of the highwater mark holds exotic seeds or plants from far upstream. Sometimes a live tree will be swept downstream, its bank-clinging roots finally pried loose by the insistent fingers of the churning water. It becomes a haven for a new community of animals in its changed neighborhood—a natural mobile home. We also have the chance to see the amazing tangled structure of roots where trees have

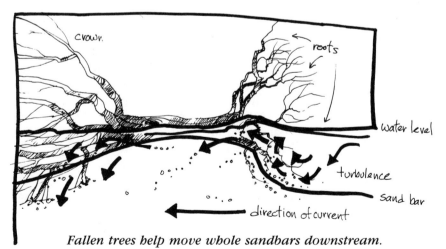

Fallen trees help move whole sandbars downstream.

Field journal page. Leaves and twigs are down after a windstorm.

been wrenched from the earth. Notice their form to appreciate fully the great earth anchors under the upright trees.

You may find a new island in a stream after a major flood; silt and fine sand has been deposited here in the wake of some upstream obstacle. Be careful. For the first few weeks after high water, the almost microscopic sand of which they are formed may still be extremely wet, suspended in a viscuous solution: quicksand.

Look closely; you may find the exposed homes of small mammals. Even a fox might have made its home under a now-fallen tree in the woods.

TORNADO

A still more devastating storm is the awesome and mesmerizing tornado. The cyclonic winds in one of these swirling, vertical dervishes may be three hundred miles per hour, enough force to drive apart the fibers of a living tree and shoot a cotton rag through the aperture. Entire freight trains may be lifted like Lionel models and deposited hundreds of yards away. Virtually nothing is safe in this storm's direct path. We watched as one approached the park, ripping trees from the ground like a gardener pulling weeds. It towered over the hill, connecting heaven and earth with its twisting, destructive rope. Then, just before the town would have been hit it bounced once, twice—and then lifted directly overhead.

As amateur naturalists, we can study the results of such storms and record their destruction. They may be frightening, but they are also fascinating. Storm-chasing scientists are learning more about what causes such storms to occur, the better to give those in their path adequate warning. Downdraft (wind shear) seems to be a factor, as does temperature and air pressure. The familiar wall cloud marching across the sky is a warning sign to all who live in "Tornado alley."

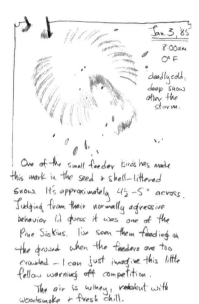

Jan. 3, '85
8:00am
0° F
deadly cold,
deep snow
after the
storm.

One of the small feeder birds has made
this mark in the seed + shell-littered
snow. It's approximately 4½–5" across.
Judging from their normally agressive
behavior I'd guess it was one of the
Pine Siskins. I've seen them feeding on
the ground when the feeders are too
crowded — I can just imagine this little
fellow warning off competition.
  The air is wincy, redolent with
woodsmoke + fresh chill.

*After a snowstorm we can find clues
to our feeder birds' identities in the
snow.*

WINTER STORM

Winter can be deadly to small birds and mammals. After a deep snow, seeds may be bent and hidden from the hungry birds. Water supplies are frozen (although I have watched birds eating snow for moisture). Small mammals just heavy enough to break through the snow's crust may have difficulty finding their customary foodstuffs or even their own burrows in the newly changed landscape. Their tracks will tell the tale, if you follow them far enough. You will be able to see where a rabbit has dug beneath the snow to find a bit of frosty greenery, or where a squirrel has excavated a dimly remembered cache.

This is the time to make sure your garden birds have ample supplies of seeds and grain. Plenty of rich, fatty sunflower seeds or chips will keep the fire of life in a small, stepped-up metabolism. In really brutal weather I make sure my birds have suet and a supply of warm water, changed often to keep it from freezing. I often see visitors that would otherwise never deign to frequent such a cozy, domesticated "bird café."

A bit of grain (corn or wheat) and nuts will keep squirrels, mice, and other small mammals alive and well during particularly vicious weather. These animals generally will have seen to their own needs during their fall storage forays, but when snows are deep they might not be able to get to their cache.

Even deer might need our help to survive long periods of deep snow. Grain, hay, or cut, tender branches may tempt them to your park or garden if you live on the edge of town.

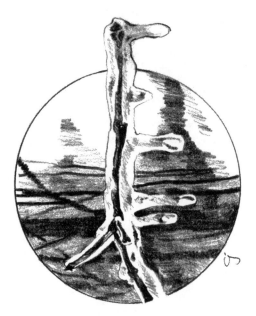

Twigs, buds, weed seeds, and other natural sources of food are encased in an impregnable coat of ice. Unless it thaws quickly or we respond with stepped-up feedings, many birds and small mammals may starve.

ICE STORM

The night is silent with a rustling, whispering silence. On top of the pale snow a freezing rain is falling, coating each branch, twig, exposed blade of grass, seed head, and weed with glass-hard frozen crystal. Later, in the night, we may hear the crack and boom of falling branches as the weight of the ice becomes too much for the trees to bear. The devastation of an ice storm rivals that of a tornado and is often more wide reaching. An entire state may feel the frigid grip as everything is locked in icy, deathlike beauty.

Warm air in an upper layer of the atmosphere (warm to just above freezing is all that is necessary) allows moisture to fall, at first as rain. Colder ground temperatures congeal the moisture as it hits. Even temperatures slightly above freezing at ground level may produce an ice storm if intervening air layers are sufficiently cold. Cold-enough air produces sleet or snow; air just on the boundary is unpredictable.

Go out after an ice storm. It is a frightening, sobering kind of beauty; when the morning sun strikes cold fire, frozen rainbows shine on each bush and twig. This is starvation time in the park and backyard. Food stores are locked away under their coating of ice, and birds and animals soon feel the pinch of hunger. Again, this is the time to see to your backyard birds and other visitors; who knows what hungry creature may visit the fallen grain under the feeder? I found a family of raccoons there one glittering winter night. They skated away across the ice, slipping and falling over each other in their haste to escape my light.

FLOODED GARDENS

Even in our own backyard we can read the aftermath of a storm. Your garden may be washed with floods of water if you live on a hill or in the lowlands of your town. Until the street department built a retaining wall uphill, my garden caught the runoff from the hills that ring our town. The storm's aftermath was interesting, if somewhat messy. Rocks and pebbles from the limestone formations on higher ground were washed across the garden in a miniature-ice-age-like scablands. Here and there tiny, snakelike zigzags where temporary streamlets meet mimic the meanderings of the flowing waters of our great rivers. My garden became a delta where the tiny rivulets run out onto the patio, carrying my hard-won soil with them. This microcosm helps me understand the forces that shaped the larger landscape. I can recognize the same shapes in a field guide for amateur geologists.

Seeds from far away may be blown or washed into your garden after a real gully washer. You may reap an interesting crop of volunteers if you allow them to sprout. Look closely: Your garden will be alive with earthworms fleeing their flooded burrows. Bumblebees cluster grumpily about the entrance to their underground home. They might be more inclined to sting when denied the refuge of their nest, so keep your distance.

Keep a record of the changes in your own backyard after a storm. Note any unusual sightings. Even here you may learn much about what is happening in the larger world. What we see on our home turf we can multiply by hundreds and thousands to get some idea of how the forces of nature in the form of storms affect our environment.

·THIRTEEN·

Every stone in the creek wears a cap of mounded snow.

Jan. 4 - "Snow Turtles" in the Creek

Winter Wanderer

Winter, to some, seems a bleak time of death and stillness, a colorless period of neutral black and white and brown. People stay indoors near a fire or hurry from place to place bundled against the cold, looking neither right nor left as they go from warmth to warmth through the icy blasts. We admire the picture-postcard world through frost-curtained windows and fight off cabin fever until we can again get outside and enjoy nature.

What can there be to see during these still, cold months that you can't watch from the cozy vantage point of your kitchen window? As we drive through the park, the land that swarmed with activity only a few months or weeks before seems as lifeless as the dark side of the moon, with the exception of a few darting squirrels and the flash of a wintering cardinal.

Even those people who enjoy traditional winter activities and sports may see the slate of outdoor life as wiped almost clean; but is it? Are the birds and animals really gone? Has growth stopped in the woods? Have all the mushrooms disappeared until spring's wet warmth brings them safe return? No, they are waiting to be discovered by hardy amateur naturalists, outdoor watchers dedicated to study and the peace and satisfaction it brings, no matter what the season.

FIRST SNOW

The warm hues of limestone rocks and oak leaves stand out warmer still against the snow's ultramarine shadows. Where the sun hits the sparkling whiteness the warm color is reflected back into the shadows, bringing them to life. Pine siskins and black-capped chickadees land on ice-covered branches with the sound of a violin being plucked, and when the wind picks up, the ice cover crackles like an open fire.

White snow is not white, visually. I walk the deserted road down hor-

jay mocking the sound
of a hawk — a pair
of them investigate
me as I draw

This jay was trying to fool me into thinking he might be a hawk instead. He never once said "jay!" all the while I sat drawing him in the cold drizzle.

izontal stripes of cold blue and pale gold where the tree shadows form a warp for the random weaving of tire tracks. Few footprints mar this still, smooth cover; mine are the only human ones. Something has crossed the road and made its way up the hill path, its prints indistinct and impossible to read after a night of strong winds. A flicker drums up on the hill, and a jay calls from across the creek with his rasping "j-jeay, jay, jay!" The wind rises, and my eyes sting as if salt had been flung into them.

The sun shines thinly and weakly through the cloud cover, a vague, rainbowed presence. When I nestle my face for a moment against my muffler, my breath steams my glasses with these same pale, prismatic colors. The world turns pink as I exhale, and then cold air restores normal vision as the lenses chill. I turn my head at the next breath and the park is briefly gilded.

Rocks in the stream wear snowcaps like the carapaces of white turtles, their edges frilled and lace trimmed with ice, the mounded tops as smoothly formed as if by an old-fashioned soda jerk.

Beneath the hillside seep that provided water all summer for the shiest of the woods denizens, who avoided the busier creekside watering hole, the water has kept the ground clear of snow. The grass sticks up like green needles from the boggy spot at the edge of the woods.

A squirrel has stitched its favorite trees together with closely spaced lines of tracks like finely worked quilting on a puffy comforter of snow. Drifts form deep cups around the base of trees, most acute on the windward side.

The fruit of the bladdernuts glows sienna against the shadows of the snow-covered hill. Where the wind has raked the north face of Siloam Mountain nearly clear of snow, the grass shows through, whiskers swept back in response to the wind: a three-day growth of beard on the frozen face of the mountain.

Warm sienna bladdernut husks whispering in the cold wind.

Rose
Hips-Dec.

*These droplet-shaped multiflora rose hips are still
brilliantly scarlet. The birds seem to relish them.*

WINTER COLORS: TRAINING THE EYE TO SEE

Winter is not just a pen-and-ink-drawing of black, bare limbs and white
snow. We often feel that because summer's green has gone and the riot
of autumn's color has faded that the color has gone out of the world—it's
not so. Even before snow blankets the ground, reflecting the blue of the
sky and turning shadows lavender, nature is flying her colors. Because
they are now more subtle and more unexpected, we must learn to seek
them out. The treasure hunt for winter's jewels is rewarded with a new
and lasting sense of beauty: the mossy trunks of damp trees against the
maroon forest shadows; the gold and orange and red upper limbs and
twigs of the willows along the creek; broom sedge's creamy sienna; the
bright berries and winter fruits—who can long for summer's ever-present,
overpowering green when winter offers such a tapestry? Sunstruck tree
limbs turn buttery against an early morning sky, bluer and deeper than
summer's bleached hue. Raspberry canes echo the color of July berries
against a background of beiges and whites, and their thorns are as vivid
as a cardinal's crest.

As an exercise in seeing, try to list all the subtleties and nuances of the
colors you see in a typical winter day in the park or backyard. Browns,
beiges, and whites may predominate at first; but soon you will notice the
deep rich greens and blue-greens of conifers; those berry canes against
the snow; the flash of warmth beneath a yellow-shafted flicker's wing; the
blood red droplets of the fruit of the multiflora rose; and the raking orange
light of the setting sun on your backyard woodpile. Mushrooms, especially
the bracket fungus so visible at this time of year, will tax your powers of
description. Striated, with green, warm brown, orange, and tan tops, they
offer contrast with blue and lavender spores. Algae grow robustly up the
trunks of trees, and lichen dots the rocks on the hill with gray green, rich
acid green, and orange. The far hills are shades of maroon, blue, and
purple. Sunrise and sunset are often spectacular in winter, as if in com-
pensation for nature's sparing use of her brighter colors elsewhere, and
what could be more spectacular than winter's aerial conflagration, the
northern lights?

Field journal drawing. Common polyporous is beautiful: soft green and tan. This one was covered with fine, velvety hairs. The black locust bean was richly colored with elegant neutrals.

If you are an artist, trained in the use of color, you may have more specific names for the colors you see; but an artist has no corner on seeing itself. Once you have become aware of the colors, whatever names you give them will remind you to look for them again and again, and winter colors will never again seem boring or depressing.

WINTER SOUNDS: BECOMING SILENT ENOUGH TO HEAR

We have become attuned to the sounds of nature at other seasons; the singing of birds, the chatter of squirrels, the keening of the hawk, the rush of the creek in flood. Now in winter the sounds have both diminished and intensified. There are fewer birds singing in the woods: The season for staking out territory has not yet come; last year's mates have been won and families raised; many have gone South. Except for the voices of those birds that overwinter, the park and garden are now much more silent. The creek is often wrapped in ice, stilling its characteristic summer song but giving it a chuckling, whispering voice instead.

The sounds that remain seem precious because, like the winter colors, we must seek them out. In the bare woods they are intensified. Unmuffled by the acoustic canopy of leaves, they carry farther; sounds bounce from hill to hill, making it difficult sometimes to tell where they are coming from at all.

Jay scrunched up against the freezing drizzle - he looks around, swivelling his head, neck pulled in, crest down.

Now has feeling, doing his musical Tool ool call

The blue jay winters over. His variety of calls, whistles, and raucous "jay-jay" sounds make the woods seem more populated than it is now. The starlings' amazing vocabulary adds to the winter sounds.

Bird and animal sounds are fewer in deep winter. Except for the owls, whose mating and territorial sounds are heard in January and February, most bird calls are stilled. Jays still slice the air with an occasional raucous sound, and their musical "tool-ool" call brightens my day. Starlings, festively dressed for winter in iridescent, white-dotted black, their legs pink and their beaks yellow in preparation for mating season, mutter, whine, sing, and croak with crazy abandon.

Chickadees, tufted titmice, and nuthatches with their funny metallic "beeps" in various frequencies all hold their winter conversations among themselves or scold me for intruding on their feeding territory. Pine siskins are heard more than they are seen in the park, the opposite of their silent, single-minded ranks at our backyard feeder.

When I bend to hear, the creek talks to itself with a hollow chuckling sound, voice disguised by the ice. Up the hill, dressed in ice spangles, the tiny waterfall has a faraway sound as if heard in a dream.

Even the squirrels have curtailed their usual chattering and scolding. They are older now and perhaps wiser; less curious about this odd two-legged beast who dares to put an acorn or two in her pocket. In September and October this was a cardinal offense to the squirrels, who responded to my "pssh-h-t" call with great threats of mayhem, drumming the tree trunks with their front paws and flashing their graceful tails at me like angry angoras. Now they disappear furtively behind the trunks as I approach, flattening themselves guerrilla style against a limb. It takes a sharp eye to differentiate a squirrel from the proverbial bump on a log.

Winter is a good time to be silent ourselves, to listen. I sit quietly for as long as possible, picking out the winter sounds. A squirrel, hidden in its winter apartment, scratches its big teeth against a nutshell with the unnerving sound of chalk on a blackboard. A pair of trees grown too close together in the woods creak and groan as they rub against each other, a giant's fiddle and bow. The smaller twigs rattle in the wind, particularly if an ice storm coats them with its hard, transparent resonance.

*Field sketchbook page. The squirrels
are much shier than they were only a
month ago—older? wiser? or just
feeling more exposed with their dense
leaf cover gone?*

It is difficult to become quiet enough to hear all a winter's day has to
offer. We are used to a cacophony of sounds carefully screened by our
inner computer to allow only those we need to hear to penetrate. Now
we are in the position of allowing all sounds to make themselves known.
Allowing the mind to become silent and letting the world speak to you
on its own terms is a contemplative exercise. Listen to your own breath-
ing. Let it become quiet and measured. If your thoughts are chaotic or
you have a number of stresses, now is the time to let them go, also quietly.
By allowing these sounds to penetrate our usual inner chatter, we become
a part of nature and we allow it to become a part of us.

DEATH, HIBERNATION, REBIRTH

Winter seems still and dead because we don't realize there is a beehive
of activity that hums away under the surface. *Beehive* is an apt-enough
metaphor, by the way; honeybees do winter over, a milling, humming
mass protecting the queen in its center. Stored reserves of honey provide
rich sustenance for the long months when no flowers bloom, and bees in
the center of the mass take turns with those on the perimeter—a very
democratic society in this way at least.

Many insects die when the air becomes chilled and the flowers go, but
even those insects that normally have short life spans will have made
provisions for the future in eggs carefully laid by for the warming days of
late winter and spring or in closely woven chrysalis overcoats to protect
them from the winter. In January or February, a mild day may bring out
a sluggish mosquito or a gnat benumbed by cold. The young bumblebee

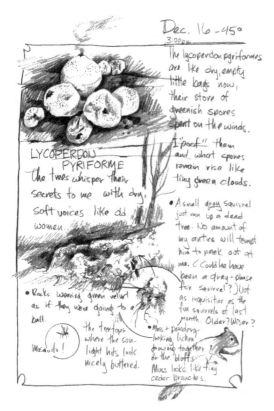

Dec. 16 -45°
3:00 pm

The lycoperdon pyriformes are like dry, empty little bags now, their store of greenish spores spent on the winds.

I "poof" them and what spores remain rise like tiny green clouds.

LYCOPERDON PYRIFORME
The trees whisper their secrets to me with dry, soft voices like old women.

• A small gray squirrel just ran up a dead tree. No amount of my antics will tempt him to peek out at me. (Could he have been a gray-phase fox squirrel?) Not as inquisitive as the fox squirrels of last month. Older? Wiser?

• Rocks wearing green velvet as if they were going to a ball.

the treetops where the sunlight hits look nicely buttered.

Mosquito!

• Moss + powdery-looking lichen growing together on the bluffs. Moss looks like tiny cedar branches.

Field sketchbook page. As late as mid-December or as early as a warm day in January or February I may see a sluggish mosquito in the park or the backyard. They are either males or not hungry; I am never bitten at this time of year. October's puffballs are puffing their spores out, a cloud of future mushrooms.

queen survives the cold months underground alone, waiting for spring's mitigating warmth to replenish her colony. Some insects hibernate, digging themselves into the insulating mud at creekside like the toads, frogs, and crayfish that populate summer evenings. Naturalists once believed in the theory of spontaneous generation; frogs, toads, and insects of all kinds were thought to rain from heaven in the spring, full grown and hopping.

Look under the bark of dead and dying trees to find the winter sleeping places of bark beetles and other wood borers. (Watch where flickers and woodpeckers hammer—they may be in search of this rich source of protein.) A January thaw may bring little piles of sawdust on the snow, telling you of a wood borer's unseasonal activity.

Mammals in the park have their own resources for winter. Few actually hibernate in my section of the country, but some have a kind of twilight sleep from which they waken, eat from their stores of food, and drowse off again. Hibernation is a kind of dormancy not unlike that of plants and trees; the life force is withdrawn to the center, body temperature drops, and energy is conserved. No food is taken in true hibernation.

Little brown bats, busy with their insectivorous activities all summer, went to earth for the winter sometime in October; females first, males and young somewhat later. They've left the park and neighborhood street-

Woodchucks and their den chamber.

lights for the limestone caves near the river, winter home for generations of night fliers. These small creatures will travel as far as 150 miles to reach the family wintering spot, where they become as cold as the stone of the cave walls. They may rouse, but only briefly, from their winter sleep when temperatures rise or lower too radically from the optimum hibernating range, when body fluids become depleted, or when bladders fill uncomfortably—not so very different from ourselves on a long winter's night.

The woodchuck that furtively waddled across the road near the big pine and looked back at me indignantly when I followed him in August's heat has also gone to earth for the winter; he is one of the few larger mammals that actually hibernates here. He built his own burrow (rather than taking over the old den of another species as many less particular mammals do) in the overgrown banks of the creek just below where I saw him last.

The chipmunks of the park indulge in various degrees of hibernation (for them more of a torpor, really). The thirteen-lined ground squirrel is the only one of these small, gnawing mammals that truly hibernates.

The flowers and butterflies of the milder seasons might have disappeared, but that doesn't mean all are dead. Mourning cloak butterflies have only suspended their mourning, hiding over winter from the cold under the bark of trees or between the shingles on the shelter-house roof; or perhaps in the eaves of my house. They are the only butterflies here that actually hibernate. Other tortoiseshell butterflies that hibernate live north or west of my area.

Mourning cloak butterfly.

Under the soil, next year's spring beauties are living on the starches stored in their tiny underground bulbs. Onionlike in form, these bulbs contain all that is necessary for new flowers, in miniature. Other flowers overwinter in roots and rhizomes or in their hard seeds; they are specifically suited to withstand the rigors of winter by long evolution. Each seed is a viable new life, a miracle needing only soil, warmth, and moisture to begin the cycle of root, stem and leaf, blossom, fruit, and back to seed again (along with a bit of luck to avoid being eaten by some small mammal or wintering bird, although that often suits a flower's needs as well. Traveling far and wide in the creature's digestive system, the hard seed may finally be deposited, unscathed, in a new and uncrowded habitat).

Hiding beneath the bare soil with its scant covering of dead grasses, root systems are alive and waiting patiently for spring. The spores of mushrooms have floated through the air to hospitable homes on dead and dying wood or other forest litter. Threadlike mycelium, the vegetative part of the fungi, hides like a fairy's macrame just under the leaf mold; the stuff of spring's fruiting bodies. Deep in the soil the earthworms slowly tunnel, enriching the earth with their castings.

Trees may look bereft of life in the winter months, but look closely: Next year's buds have already formed, tightly jacketed in their various coverings. Some look like spear tips, others like small, closed pinecones. Open one of these buds and you will find the tender green of spring. The sap will flow on the first warm days of February and March, and soon after the buds will begin to open in the woods and backyards.

INVISIBLE ACTIVITY

Much is going on in the winter woods that we do not see. We may not know where or how to look; we may be out and about at the wrong time of day. A bit of education on how to read the signs may be all that we

During winter, fox squirrels wreaked havoc on the park's slippery elm population and made serious inroads on maples and even a few oaks. Tiny teeth marks were everywhere on the stripped branches.

The park's nocturnal raccoons leave tiny handprints near the creek.

need. A bare spot on a tree limb shining against the gray bark tells us a squirrel has been busy dining on the phloem and cambium under the corky bark. On closer inspection, teeth marks confirm this diagnosis. A tree near the creek, chewed to a point close to the ground, says that beavers have gone about their nocturnal business stocking their lodge or rebuilding a section of dam. In our area young trees need to be protected with chicken-wire stockings to keep the beavers from destroying too many in the park.

The best time to look for tracks in the park is after a light snow. Snow makes as good a medium for reading sign as the mud at creekside; better, actually, since the snow covers a much broader area. If it is not so deep that it obscures the shape of the track you will be able to tell whether a fox, a coyote, a deer, a squirrel, or a cottontail has been traveling your way. Signs of a fox's nocturnal wanderings can be distinguished from numerous neighborhood dogs' tracks, although similar in shape because of their common canine heritage. The fox's habit of walking in a straight line instead of a dog's double-line walk gives it away. Canine tracks are easy to distinguish from felines', incidentally. The cat's retractable claws will not show in its tracks where a member of the dog family leaves evidence of toenails: small indentations at the end of each toe mark. This holds true for house cats, bobcats, pumas, or any member of the cat family.

Although activity is much slowed by lower temperatures, mycelium, bacteria, and moisture are going about their work of breaking down leaf mold and digesting dead and dying wood. If these processes were not somewhat active even during the winter months, the forest floor in spring would look just as it does in the fall; covered with a dense layer of crisp dead leaves and twigs. Instead, the leaf mold layer will be deep and rich, nature's compost heap at work turning decaying matter to black humus.

Moles and voles are active during the winter. Even on cold days when the soil seems too hard to excavate with a shovel, I have seen the long ridges of the mole's underground subway. Plates of frozen soil looking

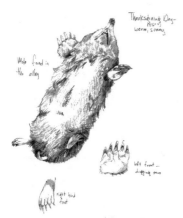

This poor mole didn't make it to deep winter—a run-in with one of the park's predators or simply a road kill. His brothers were still tunneling in January.

much too heavy for this small mammal to lift are stacked and jumbled like the earth's own plates along the San Andreas fault. One year when the ground was protected by snow for many weeks, the moles tunneled half in soil and half in snow. When spring thaw came it took a bit of puzzling to figure out the little scooped depressions in the hard earth, which looked as if someone had dragged something heavy in a crazy random pattern, until I realized the top half of the tunnel must have melted away.

The vole's tunnels are supported by a superstructure of grass blades and weed stems, often covered over by snow. In the spring when the snow is rotten and wet it will collapse on the tunnels, exposing a maze of incredible complexity.

Bark beetles will have left their maps and mazes as well, just under the bark of dead or dying tree limbs or fallen logs. You can identify the type of beetle by the map it has drawn and deduce clues as to its name by the type of tree it prefers. Ash bark beetles and spruce bark beetles, obviously enough, prefer those trees from which they take their names. The engraver beetle will leave a centipedelike mark, most often on fruit trees, and the oak bark beetle tangles his lines like a skein of yarn found by a kitten.

Bark beetle's calligraphy.

Baltimore oriole's nest.

Winter is a good time to inspect the activity invisible during the summer in the heavy cover of leaves or brush. Birds' nests are easily visible and fun to identify from their shape or position in the tree. Orioles hang tightly woven bags like socks on the clothesline from the branches of large trees. Hummingbirds' tiny, cuplike nests are often close to the ground. Look to see what the birds have used to build the nest with for a clue to the builder's identity. Many birds, of course, are opportunists; they'll use what's available. One of my favorite finds from this summer was a festive nest made with gift-wrap ribbon.

Be advised that it is against federal law to bring home a bird's nest, especially during the nesting season. You could receive a heavy fine or at least a reprimand. Be sure to ask permission for such a collection, and do it only during the winter in any case; not one out of a thousand birds will return to the same nest.

PATTERNS, TREE LACE, FROST, AND ICE

The park in winter is a Celtic drawing of patterns. The abstract and angular patterns of tree lace are magically transformed to glistening orbs when the sun shines directly through them. The light from a street lamp will have the same effect, striking fire from just those twigs that will form a halo around the glow of light. The lamp becomes a magician's spider, weaving straight lines into sparkling circles.

The edge of the creek is patterned with ice before the deep cold of winter freezes it solidly across; eyelet lace decorates each small inlet and rock in the shallows. When the creek has turned to ice, each new day brings a different message in crystalline runes on the surface. Nature hates to repeat herself and so astounds us with her varied magic.

Mammals have left their own random patterns in the snow in their intricately stitched footsteps. Opossums, foxes, squirrels, and cottontails have decorated the surface of the snow thoroughly two days after it fell.

The architectural design of deserted paper wasp nests is easily and safely observed now. The wasps carefully constructed ever-outward-increasing rings of hexagons during the summer from their own saliva "glue" and cellulose from the park's trees. These nests can be found on tree limbs, on bushes, in shelter houses, under porch ceilings, or in garden sheds. When empty now in winter, they may be taken inside to study. The wasps will build new ones come spring.

WINTER CLOSE TO HOME

In our backyards and gardens we have the opportunity to observe nature on an intimate scale. Birds that cared for themselves all summer and fall quite nicely, thank you, are now frequent visitors at our feeders. Watching and anticipating their feeding patterns is an education in itself. Nuthatches hang head down to feed, as they hang when insects and their larvae are plentiful in tree-bark crevices. They hop into my feeder at the last second. Downy woodpeckers mimic the much larger redheaded woodpeckers and their cousins, the flickers, hopping up feeder poles and bracing themselves with stiff tail feathers. Rascally blue jays seem intent on taking care of Number One—they scatter seed far and wide and even take morsels to hide. They might be leaving caches for a snack later, perhaps (although some ornithologists believe this is a food dispersal activity for discouraging too much competition at the feeder). Ground feeders will clean up much of the seed spilled by the messy eaters.

Multiple feeders feed more than these competetive birds. Nearly every window in my house opens onto at least one vista of feeder activity. Flat feeders, finch feeders, feeders constructed especially for smaller birds, plus open invitations to those comical scamps, the jays and starlings, in larger, more open feeders assure me of entertainment and education wherever I look.

In winter a hungry raccoon may visit your trash can or raid your bird feeders at night. Watch for its tiny, handlike tracks to identify the culprit when your garbage is strewn over the porch.

WINTER INDOORS

Nature watching moves indoors during the coldest hours, or when time or illness may keep you confined to your home. We share our homes, like it or not, with many forms of life. It's a rare home that hasn't had its share of spiders, cockroaches, silverfish, or ants. Before you reach for that can spray, watch a bit. You might learn something from these other inhabitants.

During the winter we had a mini-infestation of five-lined acrobatic ants, those tiny, red-brown, translucent creatures normally seen on the forest floor. I am, I suppose, a truly dedicated naturalist—never for a moment did I consider ant traps! This was a wonderful opportunity to learn and observe without leaving home. If given a choice between housekeeper and naturalist, my decision would be an easy one.

Winter's changes are cosmic in scope, probably too large for us to see. The days that have become shorter and shorter all fall begin once again to lengthen after December 21, the winter solstice; light begins to take over once again from the devouring darkness. The balance of power has shifted. The stars in the night sky wheel and change overhead. Trees, monoliths of the forest, grow silently, pushing their network of nutrient-seeking roots deeper into the ground. Rocks crack and split with the expansion of water frozen in their hairlike fissures on their way to becoming soil.

Becoming a winter wanderer simply requires a different way of seeing, a closer looking and listening. There is a new set of signposts to be interpreted for which we need a willingness to look beyond and within.

FOURTEEN

Young, injured turkey vulture and airborne adults.

The Noble Scavengers

To put *noble* and *scavenger* together seems almost ludicrous, a contradiction in terms. The word *scavenger* perhaps carries even more emotional baggage with it than the word *predator* does. Our prejudice against scavengers is so strong that naturalists once were ready to believe the most bizarre "facts" about the animals they observed engaging in eating rotting flesh: Vultures would rip out the eyes of a living baby. Spotted hyenas (because of the unusual genitals of the female) were hermaphrodites. Wolverines would eat until their stomachs were as tight as drum skins and then force out the food by squeezing their distended bodies between two trees so they could return to devour the rest of the carcass.

Actually, a zoologist's definition of *scavenger* is "any animal adapted to eating carrion, dung, or other dead organic matter"; such animals clean up considerably more from our environment than road-killed creatures.

Were it not for the work of our noble scavengers, we would soon be overwhelmed by rotting flesh. Vultures alone clear away up to eighty percent of the carrion on the Serengeti. In this country dead animals could quickly become a source of disease; a malodorous haze would hang over the land. In the wild many animals die of natural causes: illness, old age, starvation. Squirrels miss a step while executing their arboreal tightwire act and fall. Baby birds fall from the nest or are tossed out by cowbirds or jays. Other animals are killed by predators, and their remains are left behind to rot once the fresh meat is consumed: Perhaps the predator was frightened away, or perhaps it had simply eaten its fill and hunting had been too good to cache the leftovers for another meal.

Other animals die of what we might call natural causes but are in fact the result of direct or indirect human intervention and encroachment on what was once a finely tuned and balanced habitat. Large birds come into contact with power lines, completing a lethal circuit with their wings. We foul the streams and overfertilize the fields; runoff of effluents from our feedlots causes polluted watersheds, affecting thousands of animals downstream. Even thermal pollution is a problem. In those areas where too-warm water is allowed to drain into creeks and rivers without sufficient cooling time, many fish, reptiles, amphibians, crustaceans, and other small life forms die, floating belly up until they come to rest downstream, stinking, on the banks.

Our road kills account for a significant number of wildlife deaths—any trip down a country road or two will tell you that. It's a rare drive when we don't see at least two of these unlucky animals, flattened by cars. If we multiply that by just the number of miles of road in our county alone the numbers reach astounding proportions. Conservation commission officers are often simply too busy to attend to these road kills; there are just too many of them.

If you have been near even a small dead animal in summer a day or two after its death, you'll never forget the sickening smell of carrion. So why doesn't the countryside smell like one huge charnel house? Why aren't we confronted at every turn by the bones of the dead? The reason is that the cycle is completed by scavengers.

VULTURES

I have learned to love these huge black birds. Turkey vultures, with their wrinkled, bald red heads and glossy black feathers, are the ones most common in my area. They are a feature of my blue midwestern summer skies from childhood—a source of wonder, of awe, of laughter; of the chill of dread and superstition. Buzzards, they're called, here; the formal and correct *vulture* sounds too austere and too forbidding, like something you'd meet unawares on the searing African plain when you'd really rather not. I watch for them each spring—and spring is truly here when at last they sail the skies over the park.

Buzzards wheel and turn with magnificent economy of motion, riding the thermals of warm air rising from the valley floor. Ten . . . fifteen . . . twenty of the huge birds join the slowly turning vortex of feathered blackness, searching for a meal. Now and then one will fling itself out from the lazy turning dance, to be joined by two or three; then as if by osmosis the whole tribe oozes across the sky to the new axis to wheel again over untried territory.

Every day I watch the buzzards rise from their night roost on the hill. As the weather gets cooler, they appear later and later in the morning, waiting for warm updrafts on which to soar and glide; they are the ultimate hang gliders. Now as the cool nights slow their ascent they seldom fly before nine in the morning. Like their reptilian ancestors they need the sun to get up and about, if for somewhat different reasons. Cold-blooded reptiles cannot move until their blood warms and circulates.

"Ugly, disgusting creatures," people say. "Who'd want to look at a vulture?" Well, I have to admit they're no scissortailed flycatcher. Their bald, wrinkled heads look burned or plucked. Their beaks are well suited for tearing flesh. Up close, they do have a certain roughness. Aloft, in all their airborne grace, they are wonderful. Try looking at them without prejudice. What if you were to see that many eagles circling gracefully? You'd be amazed, awed, dumbstruck as if you'd been privileged to witness some ancient, secret rite of passage.

Black vultures, the other common vulture in the contiguous United States, have a smaller range, more southerly, than the ubiquitous turkey vulture. They are smaller birds, too, but more aggressive. According to the Audubon Society's field guide they'll often chase bigger birds from their meal of carrion.

It's been determined that the turkey vulture can locate food with a well-developed sense of smell, while black vultures cannot. Perhaps that's what makes black vultures more aggressive: They're at a disadvantage to their larger cousins when it comes to finding food. They have to see their dinner—what they see is what they get. I'll bet it's not so much the carrion they spot as the tea party of turkey vultures gathered to the feast.

BIRDS, MAMMALS, BEETLES, AND WORMS

Vultures are not our only scavengers, of course. Even they couldn't remove all the carrion from our highways, fields, and woods. Crows are efficient cleanup crews; we often see them picking at the flattened remains of an undistinguishable animal. Hawks and owls may occasionally eat carrion if hunting has been poor.

Coyotes have been known to eat carrion when nothing else is available, as have wolves, foxes, and badgers. Although they are thought of primarily as predators with a preference for fresh meat, when game is scarce they will eat from found carcasses or cached meat.

When no game is available at all, these animals have adapted by scavenging or by caching game when it is abundant. Predators must be opportunistic to make sure they have enough to eat when food is available for themselves and for their young. That's why you will sometimes hear

Someone's very seedy scat being fed on by snails — nothing goes to waste!

mulberry seeds —
raccoon scat?

Nothing is wasted.

of a fox or a coyote having broken into a farmer's hen house and killing many more birds than it was able to eat. If it had not been disturbed, it would have carried the extra birds away and cached them against future need.

The wolverine is generally a feeder on carrion, although it will kill on occasion. To feed her newborn kits, a female wolverine may cache meat up to six months and later return to her store. Since wolverines need a remote habitat, you will not normally see one of these fierce animals in your local park or backyard. They may be found in some of our larger national parks.

The larger and more visible creatures are not the only scavengers at work. Snails and slugs often dispose of decaying organic matter, whether carrion or dung. Flies settle on a carcass almost immediately in summer, and feeding larvae soon reduce it to nothing. Even maggots perform a service.

The sequential arrival of scavenging insects is an interesting study in itself and can be useful in forensic entomology. Blowflies arrive within minutes of death and lay their eggs. The maggots hatch and may crawl back out during this first wet stage of decomposition to pupate in the ground nearby or under the carcass. Hister beetles (family Histeridae) may arrive next, feeding on the carrion and laying their eggs to provide food for their larvae. Later, beetles that specialize in scavenging fur and skin arrive, leaving only the bones behind.

Many of the dung or burying beetles perform the undertaker's job in miniature. You may find the garden carrion beetle *(Silpha ramosa)* in your own backyard, feeding on the drying remains of some creature. Others of this family also lay their eggs on carrion. (These are sometimes called sexton beetles. They can bury whole small carcasses.)

Even butterflies may be found gathered on dead flesh or dung. They may be after protein in an easily drunk liquid form, which they can utilize with their long proboscis, or the salts available from this perhaps unlikely source.

*We seldom find antlers or bones in the park.
The mice and other gnawing mammals make
short work of them for their valuable minerals.*

The antlers deer shed each year fall to the forest floor, along with the bones of dead animals and birds, large and small. This valuable source of nutrients is not wasted. Small gnawing mammals such as mice and porcupines will dispose of the bony leavings; that's why you seldom find antlers in the woods and a forest animal's skull is a rarity. Nothing is wasted in nature, not even the calcium in bones. John Muir, one of our earliest naturalist explorers, said it best: "When we try to pick out anything by itself, we find it hitched to everything else in the universe." The work of scavengers may be disturbing to the more squeamish among us, but it is as necessary as birth.

NATURE'S COMPOSTERS

All of this organic matter eventually goes to make up the health of our soils. Nitrogen-rich carrion and dung are utilized, recycled into usable food by a wide variety of scavengers. The same elements that went to make up the life of the bird, animal, or insect that became carrion are now available to provide new life. They feed and nourish the creature that eats them, and they pass through its digestive system to become available once again to the plant kingdom, which in turn provides the necessary oxygen for the animal kingdom. Even tiny microorganisms in the soil are at work breaking down dead organic materials into their simpler, more usable forms.

Take a look at your backyard compost heap. Provide nitrogen in the form of decaying organic matter: manure, the entrails of the fish you caught, a mouse that had a run-in with your cat. Decaying plant materials will do as well if they are sufficiently high in nitrogen to stand in for our experimental carrion.

If enough moisture is present and the weather is warm enough, microbiological action will soon make the inside of your heap too hot to sustain all but the most adaptable life. Look at the edges of the heap, though, and

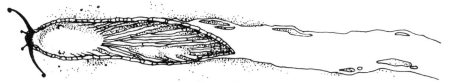

Silver trails mark the slug's passage. These, too, are efficient scavengers.

near the bottom: The active work of composting is going on here. Earthworms are busy in this cooler zone, as are tiny flies, pill bugs, slugs, roaches, and a variety of flying and crawling insects. This is a natural process that goes on even without your intervention, one you have only speeded up by a somewhat more scientific approach than that taken by nature.

BACK IN YOUR OWN BACKYARD

If you can overcome a natural aversion to decay, you will be able to learn a great deal about the work of scavengers, even on your home turf. A neighbor's dog might leave a present on your lawn; look at it a day or two later to see what it has attracted. Move it aside with a stick to see what might have invaded it from below. A variety of small insects and their larvae might be present. Leave your find a few days or a week, and it will have become a part of the soil, naturally and without your intervention.

In most areas of the United States, you may find tumblebugs at work, ridding your lawn of unwanted manure. These members of the family Scarabaeidae roll a ball of dung for some distance in much the same way a child rolls a wad of clay, perhaps to compact and further round it. The female lays a single egg inside and covers the dung ball with a layer of earth to provide a home and food for her young. These beneficial insects have royal blood. In Egypt the sacred scarab was revered for its association with rebirth, and its image was placed in the tombs with mummies to assure an easy passage to the next life.

Wood lice at work.

Egytian Scarab with Green June Beetle (Scarabaedae)

A bronze scarab image with his real-life counterpart, a member of the family Scarabaedae.

If you find a bone while digging in your flower garden, notice that the rich, nourishing marrow will long since have been scavenged by some hungry creature. If the bone had not been buried, chances are that the gnawing shrews and mice would have made short work of it for the minerals it contains. Add it to your compost heap, and it, too, will eventually disappear in a kind of natural legerdemain.

INSIDE THE HOUSE

Although you might not like to think of your home as a habitat for scavengers, chances are they are present here as well. The lined acrobatic ants that seem to find their way into our home winter and summer will do away with anything else in their path; dead water bugs, pill bugs, even a spider may be recycled by these small "gleaners."

I'm not suggesting that you become less of a housekeeper than you normally are for the sake of study, but once in a while leave a piece of organic matter (dead bug, bit of spilled meat, the residue of your cat's dinner) to see what happens.

Possibly roaches may carry away these remains. Of the nearly four thousand species of cockroaches known, most have finely developed food preferences. Some eat only fungi, some the fine hairs on plant stems. According to William Bell, professor of entymology at Kansas University, the four species that have learned to share our living quarters have acquired an impressive array of scavenging skills: They're not picky.

These roaches carry away almost anything in the form of food, and even some things we wouldn't associate with food (glue, paper). If it weren't for our natural aversion to them and for their messy droppings, we might almost consider them allies. We can at least consider them fascinating adversaries.

FIFTEEN

X *marks the spot on* Hyla crucifer*'s back.*

Fish, Reptiles, Amphibians, and Other Creatures

Although birds and mammals seem to grab the lion's share of our attention, there's a whole other world slithering, hopping, waggling, swimming, and creeping along in our parks and backyards. The waters of our parks are a wonderful breeding ground for fish, frogs, turtles, and salamanders. In the frozen mud of winter these creatures wait in suspended animation for the mitigating breath of spring. Unlike the birds and mammals they are cold-blooded creatures; their body temperature is regulated by the climatic temperature. They must wait until the sun rises high enough in the sky, warming the soil and triggering their reemergence in the park.

AMPHIBIANS

One of the first sounds of spring, in the Midwest and in much of the southeastern United States from Florida to Texas, is the welcome singing of spring peepers. It's a joyful sound. It brings joy to the listener: Winter has passed and the soft breath of life has returned. It's hard not to think of those tiny one-and-three-eighths-inch frogs having survived the winter and lived to mate again, singing a belated "joy to the world!"

The spring peeper's scientific name is *Hyla crucifer*. *Hyla* means tree frog, a family name shared with a number of other small, burrowing, hopping, and climbing frogs. The specific name *crucifer* is for one who carries a cross. The glad sound the spring peeper makes certainly belies our mournful expression of "having a cross to bear." Some say its voice, joined in chorus with many others, sounds like distant sleigh bells; it is closer to a high whistling, for me.

The female lays her sticky eggs singly in shallow water. They adhere to plant stems until warming water causes them to hatch into tiny packages of voracious hunger. Filelike rasps on their tiny lips let tadpoles scrape their dinner of protozoa and algae from underground debris, and they develop quickly, absorbing their tails and growing miniature legs instead. Fly-sized frogs leave their watery home to set up housekeeping in the weeds and trees. In my park I see them crossing the dirt path in ones and twos, unbelievably small and perfect frog microcosms. One sat immobile in my palm until my warm breath startled it; it arced away in a most spectacular leap a hundred times its own length and landed, unharmed and blinking, by the path.

In our area we may see bullfrogs, leopard frogs, cricket frogs, pickerel frogs, and wood frogs, but spring peepers are, in many ways, true microcosms of these creatures in their amphibious life cycle and choice of food. They are also preyed upon by many larger animals—including bigger frogs. Unintentional cannibalism often occurs when larger frogs see movement, which identifies prey: They're not picky. If it moves and fits in the mouth, they'll eat it.

Powerful legs allow toads to get around the park or the backyard speedily; this one took up residence at my house.

Toads have fat bodies and short, powerful legs—much less streamlined than their frog relatives. They don't need to be so streamlined, as they spend much of their lives on land. Their beautiful trilling is a magic trick of ventriloquism; it's often difficult to find the owner of the voice by following the sound. Toads may not give you warts, but they emit a stinging poison from the paratoid glands just behind the eyes. Smaller amounts of this same "predator repellent" are secreted from glands all over its body.

You may find a different amphibian in your park or your backyard if you look closely. Salamanders are often overlooked in our rambles. Nearly voiceless, these lizard-shaped creatures emit only a small squeak if picked up or threatened. Their fleshy, soft skin requires moisture, like a frog's. You'll find them near ponds and streams under moist leaf litter and in damp humus. Most of the 325 species of salamanders spend the majority of their lives on land; a few are arboreal, living in trees in more tropical climes. Some never leave the water. Others spend sightless lives in caves, never leaving their accustomed blackness; these pale creatures no longer have eyes at all. They are known as lungless salamanders, having developed feathery gills instead. The Georgia blind salamander is pure white with gorgeous red gills waving in the current like feather boas.

Newts are also salamanders. Their thick skins make ecdysis (shedding) much more visible than in their thin-skinned relatives. You may find remnants of a newt's skin on the forest floor; perhaps just waiting to go into a witch's brew.

There are many kinds of salamanders. Only their shyness and silence keeps us from being aware of their presence. Look for mole salamanders, amphiumas, mud puppies, and sirens. Look closely in the moist places; you may see one skitter away, shy of your presence.

REPTILES

Snakes are ubiquitous in my park. Turtles and lizards also abound. If you live in the southernmost states you may find an alligator or caiman in your path.

These direct descendants of the dinosaurs and other, smaller prehistoric reptiles are only a tiny shred of the evolutionary chain that was forged in ancient times. Today there is a mere fraction of the amazing array of forms of prehistory. Only turtles and crocodiles give us a clear picture, almost unchanged, of the original reptilian life forms. All the rest are more modern modifications.

In your park you may see snapping turtles (family Chelydridae), the most widespread and abundant turtles in our country. Look closely next time you see a prehistoric giant in the creek or sunning itself on a log; these are nearly identical to the earliest known fossil turtles. Look closely—

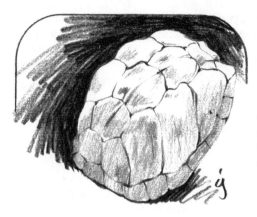

A fossilized white box turtle shell clearly shows the interlocking plates of his carapace.

but not *too* closely. Snapping turtles are extremely aggressive; unlike many of their kind who retreat to their shell for protection or turn tail and run (amazingly fast, too), these irritable creatures will lunge toward you and bite if they can. Powerful jaws and deadly accuracy make this turtle a look-but-don't-touch denizen of the park.

Common freshwater turtles, on the other hand, are fun to look at close at hand. They can bite, and painfully, but they'd really rather not. Last summer I had the opportunity to study a colorful painted turtle (painted by nature) that wandered down the middle of my street on his annual migration. It was a male; his plastron (underside) was concave to allow him to mate without falling off the female's back.

You may find a scrape near the pond or the stream where a turtle has laid her leathery eggs. Let it alone and miniature turtles will emerge as late as September to begin the cycle all over again; that is, if no predator has found the nest in the meantime. Turtle eggs are popular with raccoons, skunks, and a number of other streamside hunters.

Cooters and sliders are common sights in my area. They often land in the water with an audible "plop!" when I startle them.

Lizards populate much of our country, too. Where you live you may see a blue-tailed western skink on a stone wall; a short-horned lizard (also known as horned toad) in arid regions; a gecko in the warmer climes. You may even find a glass lizard and mistake it for a snake; it has no legs at all.

Many people have an irrational fear of snakes. Perhaps it is the serpent's bad press from the Garden of Eden or simply the fact that they are so totally, irreconcilably reptilian, so different from us—but I find them fascinating, helpful, graceful, sinuous, beautiful—and yes, a *bit* frightening.

A snake's habit of swallowing food whole is disconcerting to us. Those great jaws are engineered to become disjointed to accommodate prey that is larger in diameter than the snake. We can track the progress of the hapless creature through the snake's digestive system by the telltale lump

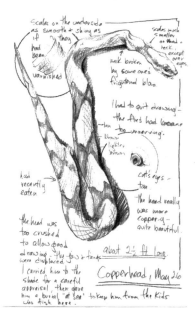

Field journal page. Copperhead found near the creek.

on an otherwise wonderfully streamlined body. Evolution has suited snakes to their niche perfectly; elongated internal organs and loss of limbs fit them well.

Most snakes in our backyards and gardens are completely harmless—to us, anyway. They are efficient predators, helping rid our environment of small rodents and many harmful insects. Garter snakes are elegant little eating machines. Common pilot black snakes, growing up to eight feet five inches in length, might look fearsome; but they are harmless, preferring to go their own way. Racers might startle us, zipping away through the grass, but they mean us no harm and in fact instinctively try to get as far away from us as possible. These are members of the family Colubridae. A great majority of the nonvenomous and only slightly venomous snakes belong to the 270 genera of this family.

CRUSTACEANS AND MOLLUSKS

Your park may have a number of mollusks and crustaceans if it has a source of water. Almost all crustaceans are aquatic (except for oddities like pill bugs and millipedes). Look for lobsterlike crayfish in all sizes. Their claws range in size from just less than one-half inch to two inches— I've seen both larger and smaller.

You may see fairy shrimp, tadpole shrimp, scuds, and copepods; take your hand lens. These small creatures are seldom more than an inch long, and copepods top out at one-tenth of an inch.

Crayfish, on the other hand, may be five inches long or more. Hatch-

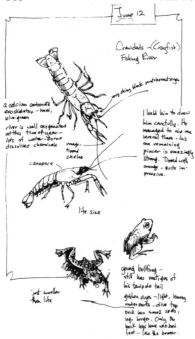

Field journal page. Crayfish and young bullfrogs share habitat.

lings are so tiny they are transparent. Crayfish are considered delicacies in our southern states; Cajun cooking abounds with crayfish recipes. Look for crayfish scudding backward under rocks or into their solitary burrows in marshy areas or wet fields.

Anyone with a garden, a damp spot in the backyard, or a source of water in a park may have seen literally hundreds of mollusks. Snail shells litter the paths in the park or hide under leaf mold. You might see a live snail traveling along by way of its muscular "foot" or feeding on garden plants, a dead animal, or droppings. (See chapter fourteen.)

Clams are found throughout North America and are an important food source for many mammals. In the state park near my home the lake level was lowered this year for work on the man-made beach. Thousands of clam shells—pearly mussels, paper shells, pill clams, and sphere clams—were exposed on the muddy banks, and this year the herons, cormorants, killdeer, and terns feasted.

FISH

No natural history book would be complete without mention of fish. These secretive, silvery creatures excite our imagination with an air of mystery. Extracting oxygen from the water as they filter it through their gills, surviving under the ice, returning to ancestral waters to spawn, leaping into the air after a mayfly, and eluding our carefully baited hooks, fish continue to amaze us.

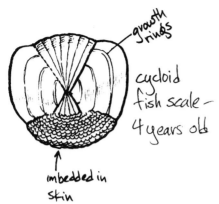

growth rings

cycloid fish scale —

4 years old

imbedded in skin

Fish scale—about seven times normal size.

You may see an American brook lamprey in a trout stream or pond. These primitive fish have cartilage skeletons instead of bone, along with circular, unjawed mouths lined with rows of rasping teeth.

More "normal" are the fish with bony skeletons. Their tiny, overlapping scales are like miniature fingernails, embedded in the skin; look at the scales closely through a hand lens or a microscope. Spiny-rayed sunfish and others commonly have cycloid scales, smooth at the rear; soft-rayed fish like trout have ctenoid scales, spiny at the rear.

Treelike, fish scales have rings that can be counted to give a fish's age. Rapid summer growth results in widely spaced rings, while a slowed metabolic rate in winter results in closely spaced ones.

Check with your state conservation commission to find out which fish are common where you live. In the Midwest we have several species of bass, carp, crappie, sunfish, minnows, and shiners. In other parts of the country you may find lake sturgeon, gizzard shad, mosquito fish, and muskellunge; rainbow, brown, or brook trout; and salmon (also a trout family member), suckers, chubs, and gars.

Among the fish commonly found in our streams, ponds, and rivers, the catfish is surely one of the strangest. Hugging the muddy bottom, this bewhiskered, big-mouthed carnivore strikes terror into the hearts of lesser fish. The tiny madtom catfish (five inches long) can inflict a painful wound with venom glands attached to pectoral fins. Others are huge and belligerent. A small boy with one of these on his hook must have thoughts of Jonah.

Stranger still are the spoonbill or paddlefish, denizens of an Ozark river in my area. They can attain great size, as much as six feet from tail to the end of their cartilaginous "bill"—no wonder they have been mistakenly described as a new species of shark. They are gentle fish, really, feeding on plankton and small crustaceans strained from the water by elongated gill rakes. Their specific name is *Polyodon spathula,* and they are like an evolutionary bridge to primitive fish; they have cartilage-bone skeletons. Only one other species of Polyodontidae is known to exist: *Psephurus gladius* makes its home in the Yangtze River valley in China.

Paddlefish

Paddlefish have a cartilaginous snout that gives them their common Missouri nickname: spoonbill.

The fish of my small-town park have spent the winter in their own kind of suspended animation. If the creeks, ponds, and lakes of the park are ice bound they will have slowed their metabolism, reducing their need to feed or even to move around. I wonder that ice fishermen are able to catch anything at all!

Come spring, when the ice breaks and the water warms, the first hungry sunfish will make their presence known with a vengeance. The surface of the water will be ringed with a thousand circular ripples of feeding fish.

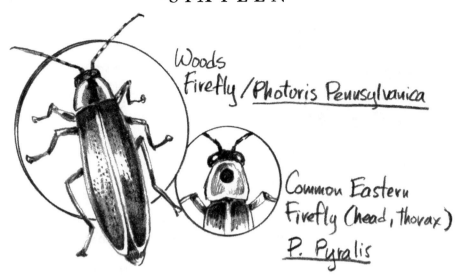

SIXTEEN

Woods Firefly / Photoris Pennsylvanica

Common Eastern Firefly (head, thorax)
P. Pyralis

You may find the woods firefly in the park; in other areas the spotted common eastern firefly is more numerous.

A Naturalist's Nightlife

Step into the park or your own backyard at night and you enter (to borrow Castaneda's phrase) "a separate reality." The experience is literally as different as night and day. New animals, nocturnal creatures, roam the paths and go about their business, their eyes well suited to the monochromatic, moving shapes of darkness, their ears tuned for the slightest sound. They move silently on catlike feet.

The air is still, expectant. It is dusk, May, and the first crickets are tuning up their lovelorn calls. Frogs sing up the creek and in the slough; spring peepers, still, and leopard frogs; and the startling bassoon of a bullfrog almost underfoot. The first mosquitoes are out; the females making a late dinner of my arms and neck.

The first lightning bug, a woods firefly *(Photinus Pennsylvanica)* sends his coded signal out to attract his ladylove; she, in the grass, answers with the enzymelike chemicals that produce a "cold" fluorescentlike light—but a warm glow in her suitor's heart, presumably. On this quiet night they consummate their nuptials in peace. On another night they may be pursued by scientists intent on divesting them of their light organs for use in biochemical assays. Other dangers lurk in the darkness for unsuspecting fireflies; not only must they beware of scientists and big-mouthed, hungry nightjars, but also the male may be lured to his death by a femme fatale intent on a late-night snack.

WHIP-POOR-WILL
on the ground

The whippoorwill's Latin name, Caprimulgus vociferus, *gives away its tendency to sing far into the night.*

Sounds are accentuated in the growing darkness—a whippoorwill tunes up halfway up the hill; it makes the sweetest sound and the saddest. Childhood night hikes come back with a nostalgic pang: We always listened first for the sound of the whippoorwill, on her nest near the ground, large eyes alert and rounded wings folded. This one is close enough for us to hear the "click" at the beginning of each "whip-poor-*will,* click, whip-poor-*will.*" Is it her indrawn breath? Where you live you may hear the chuck-will's-widow or the poorwill instead—these members of the nightjar or goatsucker clan like well-leafed forests, river woodlands, pine woods, isolated groves of trees, or even dry hills and open brushy areas. With this wide range of habitat types, you should hear some member of this family where you are.

Tree limbs are silhouetted against the night sky. In full dark the sky is still the light giver; the trees cast their shadows on the road even on a moonless night. We navigate pools of light, deep holes of shadow.

Pale limestone rocks glow phosphorescently in the moving, inky water of the creek. Our eyes are beginning to adjust to the grays instead of colors and wide-value ranges.

The scent of leaf mold and trees; the rich algal smell of still water, redolent and evocative; the quick musk of a faraway skunk, almost pleasant in the distance—smells are much more noticeable in the cooling night air. You can locate wild grapes by the almost sickeningly sweet pockets of scent. Perhaps it is only that my other senses are beginning to take over from my nearly useless vision.

At last we shine our powerful light up into the trees and are treated with a magical sight. Hundreds of points of sparkling green light shine back at us: spiders' eyes.

If this stretches your credibility, drive slowly on a country lane at night. If you see a tiny green light wink back at your headlights on its way across the road, stop; get out; and walk slowly toward the light. A spider will be there waiting, I promise you, if you are lucky. If not, try again; you've only missed him.

Wolf Spider

*The glowing green of spiders' eyes in the night may be of the forest wolf spider (*Lycosa gulosa*).*

THE COMING OF NIGHT

Even before I can discern the difference in the light at the tail end of the day, birds and animals are becoming more active. Diurnal creatures are getting in a last feeding before bedding down for the night. Deer, woodchucks, squirrels, and rabbits like the times between day and night.

Mosquitoes become more active in the early gray morning or as the light begins to slide off to the west. When full dark falls, their feeding activity slows.

MAMMALS. Now fox squirrels hurry and scold and work their way furtively back to their homes; a loose knot of leaves in summer, a comfortably insulated hole in a tree in colder months. Chipmunks are active again in the late afternoon. They are early risers who like to rest during the hottest part of the day and then return to activity with the coming of evening. You may see them filling their cheek pouches with seeds and nuts. Watch closely, and you will notice how judiciously they bite off any sharp points before storing their finds in those expandable fleshy cheeks.

In the fall you may see the normally nocturnal beaver at work in protected areas as night begins to fall. There's much work to be done gathering winter stores and building new dams (repair work is done at any time, but most dams are begun in the autumn). We have watched a family of beavers in a nearby park for months now, cutting trees and stripping branches against the winter's cold. No wonder about the old expression "busy as a beaver": They can fell a large tree overnight and strip it completely of branches.

Harvest mice prefer to feed just after sunset, although you might see them at any time of the day or night. The grasses and wild legumes at the edge of the park provide ample snacks, usually eaten on the spot. Later in the year, a harvest mouse may stock its nest or a cache with seeds.

We see more deer in the park when we come early or late in the day.

HIND FOOT PRINT
FOUND NEARBY

I stood very still ← 4½" →
watched him eat — then he slapped the
water & swam
quickly to the
dam. I think
he was a young
one.

Beaver Pond &
Dam

November

Beavers (Castor canadensis) *were uncharacteristically busy late this November afternoon. Normally they reserve their lumbering until after sunset.*

They seem to rest at midday, like the chipmunks. Skunks and opossums are nocturnal mammals, as are raccoons. Listen for the sounds of coyotes in the park at night. These adaptable night hunters often venture into parklands.

Another night-active mammal, one that stirs unfounded fear and superstition, is the bat. These small fruit and insect eaters seldom venture too close to us (although they have been known to take up residence in the occasional attic or belfry). Vampire bats—which actually do exist—normally live in Mexico and Central America and feed mainly on the blood of birds and domestic farm animals. Unless the bats are infected with rabies, their bites are seldom fatal, but if the victim is small enough or loses enough blood due to slowed coagulation, death can result.

Other bats that seem, perhaps, a bit too interested in us (prompting the old wives' tale that bats fly into people's hair) are usually interested only in the insects that may swarm around us and other mammals. Hold still! That bat is probably only helping with your mosquito problem.

BIRDS. As night falls, the daylight-active birds—chickadees, yellowthroats, juncos, sparrows, hawks, jays, and the like—are ready for the changing of the guard. The nightly ceremony of chimney swifts swirling around their resting places and disappearing one by one seems to set the stage for the night birds. Owls, common nightjars, and whippoorwills take over the sky. Daytime's moving tapestry of arched blue, woven with the paths of hundreds of birds, is simpler now. The nighthawks ply the airways, mouths open to capture a hapless moth or mosquito.

In the crepuscular light you will see different birds and animals; the guard has changed. Nocturnal creatures are beginning to venture out, their light-gathering eyes larger than those of their diurnal counterparts. For the space of a few minutes or an hour or so, you will see the night and day shifts together, as if comparing notes on their common territory.

LATE NIGHT

A July midnight is still and nearly silent except for the sounds of insects. The insects own the night. The cricket's steady rasp is punctuated by the harsh "sc-craa-aack" of a nocturnal katydid. The hum of a mosquito drones as loud, to my straining ears, as a helicopter's rotor in contrast with the stillness.

The backyard is nearly as devoid of auditory activity as a hot July afternoon, but the garden spiders are busy rebuilding webs torn by the day's blundering humans, cats, and dogs. A lucky few had their nets torn only by their welcome prey; these small tears are easily and quickly repaired.

Webs carefully constructed "from scratch" in a single night rarely last until the next. Take a flashlight into your backyard and watch this nocturnal work, or position yourself so the web is silhouetted against a lighted window. Different types of spiders construct different types of webs; it's fun to see what form a particular web will take, and to ask yourself why. What does this spider eat? How does it hunt? How does it catch its prey? How sticky is its web? Will its owner react if I blow on the web or touch it? Is it a nest instead of a trap? Have eggs been laid? Have young hatched? What do those mite-sized little spiders eat? Questions like these and their answers, gained after patient and bemused observation and research, cured me of a lifelong, irrational fear of spiders.

Now, in my backyard, I am able to study and observe these beautiful creatures without fear, familiarity breeding not contempt but fascination. A fat brown spider, or orb weaver, hangs upside down on its silken disk. My warm breath shakes the delicate web like an earthquake, and the spider turns, alert, to investigate. Finding nothing of interest, it returns to its normal head-down position to wait for prey. If I *had* been dinner, the spider would have reacted instantly to wrap me in a quick cocoon of silk. Each night the spider replaces the old web in total darkness, the intricate, perfect design created by touch alone; amazingly, in less than an hour.

The wolf spider by the back steps has made a different kind of web, a messy sheet thrown out like a net to catch as catch can. Leaves, seeds, and bits of debris may lie on the net's surface, but the spider knows when prey hits the web. (Most wolf spiders do not spin webs but live on the ground and hunt at night, like their namesake. This one seems to have borrowed a trick from other sheet-web weavers, although it rests on, not under, the web. Perhaps it has only wandered onto another spider's web and stayed to hunt.)

Pale green Luna (Acitas luna) *is a member of the family Saturniidae.*

NIGHT MOTHS. Moths fly like the wings of night, unlike their cousins, the diurnal butterflies. They become prey to birds, bats, and hunting spiders. Their varied antennae are extremely sensitive, leading them to a mate or a source of food in the form of nectar or perhaps warning of danger. A few primitive moths have jaws and feed on pollen, but most have a long, coiled proboscis, or tube, for drinking. They don't limit their imbibing to nectar, however; a few (wobbly) specimens may have fed on the fermenting sap of trees.

Diurnal butterflies usually rest with wings erect; moths may hold theirs curled protectively around the body, thrown out like a tent flap or resting flat against a support. The brighter-colored specimens are often day flyers; more somber moths seem to prefer the night. Some, like the catocala or underwing moth, hide their bright underwings when at rest.

For sheer beauty, these largest of the nocturnal moths are unbeatable: the tailed, pale green Luna; the nearly six-inch Cecropia; the Io with its huge, staring "eyes" meant to startle a possible predator; and the spectacular Polyphemus. These are giant silkworm moths, usually seen fluttering near street lamps or your own porch light. They are so large that you might mistake them for bats. The adult moths have only vestigial mouthparts and do not feed at all; and they have no hearing organs. Their sole function seems to be to mate and lay eggs—and give pleasure to those lucky enough to see them.

Look around your own porch light on a summer night to see an amazing variety of moths, or go "mothing" in the woods at night. Hang an old white sheet between two trees near the edge of the woods or across a path (like most wildlife, moths, too, utilize this "path of least resistance"). A strong flashlight or lantern placed behind the sheet will provide the attracting light. (Perhaps you'd best alert your friendly neighborhood police if you are doing this in the park at night; there may be a curfew, or special permission may be needed. Your own backyard, of course, has no such limitations.)

OWLS. The owls of the park hunt on silent wings. Soft feathers muffle their flight so that even the largest of our common owls, the great horned, can fly overhead with only the slightest whisper of parted air. Compare this silent passage with the noisy flight of pigeons. The predatory owl must be noiseless or it would frighten away all its prey and soon become extinct.

The eyes of all owls are huge, proportionately, set forward on the facial disk in much the same position as our own. Many more photoreceptive cells allow the owl to detect movement and patterns of movement at great distances. It knows the mouse's erratic path, and the rabbit's. It recognizes the characteristic travel patterns of prey and ignores the movements of creatures in which it has no immediate interest. It sits silently and waits; listens, too. The large, slitlike ears are placed forward as part of the facial disk, hidden and protected by feathers. Their position allows the owl to concentrate all its senses on a single point; they are asymetrically placed to give the widest possible auditory range. It's no wonder the owl is an efficient predator in the night.

THE NIGHT SKY

Look up on a clear night. Now is your chance to see the bowl of heaven full of sparkling stars. On a moonless night the stars have less competition; you may see many more stars. On a hazy night you are supposed to be able to best find the major constellations, although the last star in Cassiopeia's open W eluded me even then. Often in winter the stars are their brightest. Use a good pair of binoculars (mine are old army nightglasses) or a telescope to appreciate fully what you see. A field guide or a friendly astronomer helps in locating the constellations. Watch for meteor showers and the Northern lights, too.

NIGHT HIKE

Take a night hike at any time of the year. Nearest the full moon is often the best time, as it is easiest then to find your way without resorting to man-made light.

Practice walking like a cat, rolling on the balls of your feet first and then touching the heels to the ground; nocturnal birds and animals have acute hearing as well as well-developed night vision and will start away from our noisy approach.

Become aware of the ground underfoot. Is it spongy, springy, rough, or muddy? dry and cracked? full of hummocks and tufts of dry winter grass? Do mole holes and the trenches of erosion mar the path with ankle catchers? Your careful "night legs" will stand you in good stead here.

Notice how cool air collects in the hollows. As you walk, you enter these thermal pockets and then move back into the warmth as the path goes uphill. The hollows may be full of mist or fog.

Try your recorded owl calls. Will a real owl answer this echoing "*hoo-awww*"? This night the recorded message seems too generic, too perfect—and too characteristic. The live owl on the hill calls once; it seems to have its own message and style. This owl is not interested in any canned conversation. In January or February we might call up a chorus of interested suitors.

Listen for the sounds of migratory geese, traveling at night: high and keening like snow geese or honking chatter like the Canadas. Follow their sound to tell their direction.

Watch for a spider's eyes or the activities of night-feeding mammals. Look for bats and moths, fluttering almost erratically near the light. Identify those you find near your porch light.

Step into this unfamiliar country. Now that bicyclers and joggers fill the daylight hours the night is the last frontier.

·SEVENTEEN·

Such a simple thing as a sapling springing from the fallen trunk of a dead tree is a trigger to meditation.

Sojourner in the Woods

LEARNING TO BE SILENT

In a sense we are all sojourners in the woods: seekers, wanderers, and pilgrims; seers of "visions"; dreamers of dreams. We look upon wonders in microcosm. We are dwarfed and humbled by a tree that has lived to see the dawn of our times and perhaps beyond.

The commonplace may take on an air of mystery if we open our eyes and see the truth; not what we think we see, not what we know, but simply what *is*.

Creation continues. The circle turns and turns: a Buddhist's prayer wheel, or the cycle of birth and death and decay and rebirth. It is the wheeling of one small, sentient planet through the vastness of space.

Our eyes learn to see; but what is more than that: We learn to look, to expect, and to perceive. We see what is there, what has been, and what, God willing, is to come, in these small and homely natural happenings. The miracles of photosynthesis and the regrowth of a tiny chestnut from the ravaged trunk of a dead giant give us hope, a sense that after all, it may be all right. Our ears begin to hear; but, more than that: we listen. Our minds think, and analyze, and categorize. We catalog, list, and learn. We fill our field journals with notes and observations, checking our findings against those of the experts. We also discover acceptance: opening; *being*.

157

Is this too much to expect from a small-town park or from a corner of your own backyard? In ordinary times, yes—when we wear our normal, day-to-day, surface selves, the selves who go to work or to the supermarket with equal attention to where we are and what we are doing. At other times we can become sojourners: seekers, seers, dreamers. Nature will allow us that.

TRANSFORMATION

In our exercises in tracking, in seeing, in listening, and in using all our senses, we have become something more than our everyday selves, almost without our noticing it. That anxious person who felt helpless against the vagaries of the world and life, was I once. Was it you as well?

Many of the exercises we have tried, aside from being useful to our study of nature, are time-honored methods of meditation, relaxation, and awareness. We've put them to work in the best possible place: that place that can give back to us more than we've ever thought to seek.

In learning to be silent, in allowing nature to give us what she will rather than insisting on a particular, preplanned experience, we are transformed and expectant; like children again but with a degree of wisdom as well. We have learned not just to handle ourselves well in the woods (or at the seashore, or in the desert)—we've also learned our strengths. In a world sometimes so intent on pointing out our weaknesses, from our personal insecurities (deodorant commercials) to the very real anxieties of world-wide pollution or a nuclear holocaust, we've learned a kind of power to deal with our world.

REGENERATION

Often we are tired, worn down by pressures or expectations—by life—and we want only to run away. In going to the woods, to our park, to the mountains, or to the vast, clean openness of the desert, we are running not *from,* but *to:* to a source of strength and regeneration. If knowledge is power, this is a strange power we've chosen for ourselves but a lasting one. We'll take over no giant corporations and sway no world dictators with this power we've found in nature and within ourselves. It's a different kind of power: rebirth, with each day, each time we step outside and go into the woods.

CONTEMPLATION

The Eastern mystics and the Zen masters know more of this than the Western mind may ever be able to take in, but we can take a page from their book and allow ourselves to contemplate the small beauties we find. In a Zen garden, nature is distilled: a perfect microcosm symbolizing all life. We can find our own small Zen garden in a park; a special bench with a calming view; the gnarled roots of an ancient tree, clinging to life; the humble, patient, eternal lichen on one special stone.

Contemplation is only taking the tracking, stalking, seeing exercises one step further; being silent, being open, being *there;* stalking something larger than ourselves. A few minutes spent in true contemplation have more power of regeneration than today's passing fancies of hot tubs and jogging tracks can begin to approach.

MAKING A "QUIET PLACE" AT HOME

Each of us can make a small place of peace and beauty for ourselves, in our backyards or gardens, or even on a city balcony. First, look around. Let your yard or available space speak to you. Where are you drawn? What most interests you? Where does the sun soothe the kinks from your muscles or the cooling shade give you back to yourself after a hard day? Is there a view of far hills pinched off between two houses? Does a neighbor's tree reach companionably into your yard? Find your special place; it's there. One city friend simply has a spot on a second-story porch that is washed with pale morning sun; her plants thrive, and birds frequent the feeder. It's a special place—and it's over a busy Italian restaurant; so you see, an idyllic country setting is not a necessity.

Another friend has built a deck on the second story of his home. An enormous oak grows through the redwood floor, and he lives as if in the tree.

If you have room, consider a hammock for your special place. Your backyard birds and animals will become used to your presence—so different from that of their instinctive two-legged enemies—and you may have the opportunity to observe much more natural behavior than otherwise. You will be accepted. A patio lounge will do as well as a hammock if you have no place to hang one; or buy a hammock with a standing frame.

Some kind of screening will allow you privacy, and privacy allows quiet. A fence, a folding screen, a trellis, or tall bushes along the borders will encourage quiet, your own and others'. You might even want to pitch your tent in the backyard as a kind of miniblind. In some places you may need to use your quiet place at odd hours, though—when the rest of the neighborhood is asleep or at school or work. Even a two-sided "booth" of dowels and heavy cloth will give the illusion of being alone; it's the image in our minds that's important, anyway.

If you are fond of birds, make sure you have a feeder and a source of water. The soothing sounds of water in a recirculating pump will act as "white noise" to screen out auditory distractions: a boon to you as well as to the birds.

If you like, plant an herb garden, for the scents and for the insects and butterflies that are attracted to the aromatic flowers. A rustic rock-garden style is more naturalistic, but you may prefer a formal, more traditional approach for a sense of order in your sanctuary.

If such things are meaningful to you, buy a small piece of garden sculpture, such as a Saint Francis (the naturalist's patron saint) or an oriental lantern. This will give a focus to your small sanctuary. A sundial is a wonderful choice, reminding you of the natural rhythms in the world.

If time is an important consideration—if you have very little of it to spend here—leave your watch off entirely. You'll only mar the quality of time by continually sneaking a peek to see how much you have left to spend here. Use a small alarm clock, but try to find one with a pleasant alarm and keep it out of your line of sight.

You might want to keep your binoculars or hand lens nearby, too, along with your field journal in case a verbal observation comes to mind, but I prefer to keep these times simpler, unencumbered by too many "things." A cool drink or a cup of tea is nice, though.

In short, make your quiet place as pleasant for yourself as you can. Give yourself something to look at, no matter how small: a microcosm of nature in your own backyard; a naturalist's Zen garden, Western style (*or* Eastern, if you prefer). Allow yourself to be comfortable, and give yourself permission to take the time, no matter how busy your schedule or demanding your family.

It is said that we are made up of everything we've ever seen, thought, felt, spoken, or done and on the subconscious level all of this becomes a permanent part of us, engraved in our gray cells forever.

·APPENDIX·

An Informal Bibliography and Suggested Resources

Your own study of natural history is, of necessity, a very personal thing. As you spend time outdoors, asking yourself questions, making discoveries, and digging out the answers, only you will know which field of study touches a chord with you. I am somewhat of a generalist; nearly everything that moves—and most things that don't—interests me. This bibliography reflects that.

These are only books that have meant something to *me;* I may have missed a jewel or two or forgotten to mention some. Space requires that I not list *everything*. From these few, I hope you'll find something helpful.

BOOKS FOR CHILDREN AND YOUNG ADULTS

Some of the best natural history books are intended for children and young adults; they are easy to understand, well written, and full of fascinating facts that authors of books for adults might not think to include. For the child in all of us, I recommend *The Curious Naturalist* by John Mitchell and the Massachusetts Audubon Society (Englewood Cliffs, NJ: Prentice-Hall, Inc., 1980). Beautifully designed pages by Gordon Morrison are accurate and informative. Two books by Jim Arnosky, artist and naturalist, are fun to read and to look at: *Drawing from Nature* (New York: Lothrop, Lee and Shepard Books, 1982) and *Secrets of a Wildlife Watcher* (same publisher, 1983).

A book intended for use *with* children is Joseph Bharat Cornell's excellent *Sharing Nature With Children* (Nevada City, Canada: Canada Publications, 1979). This one is full of hands-on experiences, solid information, and just plain good feeling.

GENERAL BOOKS AND FIELD GUIDES

General natural history is a roomy-enough field. Some of these books are field guides and some are storehouses of general information.

Wetlands (Audubon Society Nature Guides series, New York: Alfred A. Knopf, 1985) is one of a new series of books worth having. William A. Niering wrote this one; although each subject is not covered as comprehensively as in a separate field guide on, say, flowers or birds, having everything together in one book is handy. Another in this series is *Eastern Forests* by Ann and Myron Sutton. You should be able to find one of these guides that pertains to your own area or field of interest.

Gale Lawrence's *A Field Guide to the Familiar* "brings it home." You may never have guessed this much was going on close at hand. (Englewood Cliffs, NJ: Prentice-Hall, Inc., 1984, paper).

A very old book that lists natural events in the order they may be expected to occur is *Nature's Program* by Gaylord Johnson (New York: Doubleday, Doran and Co., Inc., 1926).

The Golden Guide paperback series from Golden Press are excellent small guides to nature. Inexpensive and well illustrated, any of these would form the basis of a beginning naturalist's collection. I still refer to them when I can't find what I am looking for anywhere else.

For a good, small general take-along book, *Nature Bound, A Pocket Field Guide* by Ron Dawson (Boise, Idaho: OMNIgraphics Ltd., 1985, paper) is fun to own. It includes information on survival in the woods as well as on edible and poisonous plants.

My favorite for plain inspiration and instruction is really too big to be a field guide; it's more of a wide-ranging compendium on being a naturalist. It's Gerald and Lee Durrell's *A Practical Guide for the Amateur Naturalist* (New York: Alfred A. Knopf, 1983). It's particularly useful in its discussion of the various types of ecosystems, including the home.

PERSONAL ACCOUNTS

Personal accounts, reflections, and experiences make up a different kind of natural history book. Often scientific at heart, these books make a personal study and invite us along.

Pilgrim at Tinker Creek by Annie Dillard (New York: Bantam Books, 1974) won the Pulitzer Prize and in doing so brought the natural history book to the attention of the wider reading public.

Signs and Seasons, John Burrough's classic book of natural history essays, has been reissued by Harper and Row (New York: 1981). It was first issued in 1886; this new edition is newly illustrated with Ann Zwinger's delightful scratch-board drawings.

Another book that has seen nearly continuous publication is *The Immense Journey* by Loren Eisely. It was first published in 1946. My copy of Eisely's classic on human evolution is from Random House (New York: 1973).

There is a wonderful new crop of natural history and scientific writers; science made fascinating and riveting. Try *Late Night Thoughts on Listening to Mahler's Ninth Symphony* by Lewis Thomas (New York: Viking Press, 1980); *The Klamath Knot* by David Rains Wallace (San Francisco: Sierra Club Books, 1984); *Earthly Pleasures/Tales from a Biologist's Garden* and *Field Days/Journal of an Itinerant Biologist,* both by Roger B. Swain and published by Charles Scribner's Sons (New York: 1981 and 1980, respectively). All are paperbacks. You may also try reading anything by Stephen J. Gould.

Any of Edwin Way Teale's books are well worth reading. Try *Circle of the Seasons* (New York: Dodd, Mead, 1953); or for a real treat, see *A Conscious Stillness: Two Naturalists on Thoreau's Rivers* (New York: Harper & Row, 1982) by Teale and Ann Zwinger. This conversation between two naturalists seeing the rivers Thoreau knew best through "modern" eyes is good reading. Of course, most naturalists have a touchstone in Thoreau himself. *Walden* is *the* classic. My copy is from the New American Library (New York: 1960).

If you enjoy Zwinger's style and her wonderful illustrations, find *Beyond the Aspen Grove* (New York: Random House, 1970)—or any of her series of books primarily dealing with the natural history of the West and Southwest.

One of my favorite books is John K. Terres's beautiful *From Laurel Hill to Siler's Bog* from Alfred A. Knopf (New York: 1969). Terres was the president of the Audubon Society for some years and writes with passion and clarity.

A recent book of personal observations of bird life is *Private Lives of Garden Birds* by Calvin Simonds (Emmaus, Pa.: Rodale Press, 1984).

John Hanson Mitchell is a wonderful writer (he did *The Curious Naturalist* and *Ceremonial Time*); this one "brings it home." See *A Field Guide to Your Own Back Yard* (New York: W.W. Norton, 1985).

Anything by the poet-writer-teacher-naturalist Wendell Berry is at the top of my list. I particularly liked *The Long-Legged House* (New York: Ballantine Books, Inc., 1965) and *A Continuous Harmony* (New York, Harcourt, Brace, Jovanovich, 1971); these are some of the first books I read that link appreciation and preservation of our environment.

A Sand County Almanac by Aldo Leopold awakened me to an ethical appreciation of nature; my copy is from Oxford University Press (New York: 1970), but the book was first published in 1949. This edition has beautiful pencil drawings by Charles W. Schwartz.

A very old book worth trying to find (a professional book search turned up my copy) is *Sharp Eyes, A Rambler's Calendar* by W. H. Gibson. Published by Harper and Brothers (New York) in 1891, this book taught me how to closely examine equisetum spores under a microscope, how to recognize wasp drones, and many other bits and pieces of esoteric natural history.

ACTIVITY BOOKS

For those who want to *do* something with nature:

Learn to track with *A Field Guide to Animal Tracks* by Olaus J. Murie (a Peterson Field Guide; Boston: Houghton Mifflin Co, 1974). This book includes birds, insects, amphibians, reptiles, bone and horn chewing, scat, and more.

Create gifts with *Earth Presents* by Beverly Plummer (New York: Atheneum, 1974) or *The Naturalist* (Minneapolis: Burgess Publishing Co., 1974).

Grow wild flowers and plants with *The Wild Garden* by Violet Stevenson (New York: Penguin Handbooks, 1985, paper), *Wildflower Perennials for Your Garden* by Bebe Miles (New York: Hawthorn Books, Inc., 1976), or *Growing Woodland Plants* by Clarence and Eleanor Birdseye (New York: Dover Publications, 1972).

Forecast the weather with *Weather,* one of the Golden Guides by Paul E. Lehr, R. Will Burnett, and Herbert Zim (New York: Golden Press, 1957); or *The Weather Workbook* by Fred Decker, a paperback from the same publisher (1981). *The Weather Almanac,* edited by Frank E. Bair and James Ruffner is a 1979 Avon paperback; a Dover Publications paperback is Frank Forrester's *One Thousand One Questions Answered about the Weather* (New York: 1982). My old favorite in the field is Alan Watt's *Instant Weather Forecasting* (New York: Dodd, Mead & Co., 1968).

EXPLORING SPECIAL SUBJECTS

WINTER. For those who love winter—or would like to: Donald W. Stokes *A Guide to Nature in Winter* covers northeastern and north central North America. It is an annotated field guide of the best sort, a hardback from Little, Brown & Company (Boston: 1976). A very personal exploration of winter is *Wintering* by Diana Kappel-Smith (Boston: Little, Brown & Company, 1984). This is a beautiful, lyrical book combining science and reflection: a must read. Or try *The Winter Woods* by John R. Quinn (Chatham Press, 1976).

NIGHT. The night is mysterious; these books make it a bit less so: *The Dark Range, A Naturalist's Night Notebook* by David Rains Wallace (San Francisco: Sierra Club Books, 1978). This paperback explores the unfamiliar territory of night in California's Yolla Bolly Mountains. Chet Raymo's *The Soul of Night* (Englewood Cliffs, NJ: Prentice-Hall, Inc., 1985) is, as the subtitle says, "an astronomical pilgrimage." *Stars,* one of the Golden Guides (New York: Golden Press, 1956) by Herbert S. Zim and Robert H. Baker is a good, clear beginner's guide to the heavens. Despite the old publication date of my copy, the Golden Guide series are always available at bookstores.

GEOLOGY. The world underfoot can be as interesting as that overhead. Fossils, rocks, and minerals tell us something of our prehistory. *A Field Manual for the Amateur Geologist* by Alan M. Cvancara (Englewood Cliffs, NJ: Prentice-Hall, Inc., 1985, paper) is a fascinating step-by-step guide for the beginning geologist. Two Golden Guides are also handy for the beginner—or anyone who simply needs to find facts quickly: *Fossils* by Frank H. T. Rhodes, Herbert S. Zim, and Paul R. Shaffer (New York: Golden Press, 1962, paper) and *Rocks and Minerals* by Zim and Shaffer (1957, paper) provide enough solid information to get anyone started.

A new book by Walter Sullivan, *Landprints* (New York: Times Books, 1984, hardbound) is stuffed with black-and-white photos and facts that lead the reader through the eons.

THE SEA. If your park is near the sea, you'll want William T. Fox's *At the Sea's Edge* (Englewood Cliffs, NJ: Prentice-Hall, 1983). As it says, this paperback's "introduction to coastal oceanography for the amateur naturalist" is illustrated with photos as well as drawings by Clare Walker Leslie.

WILDLIFE

MAMMALS. The animal lovers among us (I am one) will want guides to recognizing and understanding wildlife. My favorite is *The Wild Mammals of Missouri* by Charles W. and Elizabeth R. Schwartz (Columbia, Mo: University of Missouri Press, 1981, hardbound. First published in 1959). Don't let the title fool you—this book covers a wide variety of animals, large and small, and includes bone structure, foot construction, tracks, habits, and habitat. It's simply the best book of its kind I've seen; not a field guide—it's too big—but an indispensable reference book.

The Audubon Society Enclyclopedia of Animal Life edited by John Farrand, Jr. (New York: Clarkson N. Potter, Inc., 1982) really is encyclopedic in scope. This big hardbound book is less in depth than the Schwartz book (necessarily, given the sheer numbers of animals covered), but nearly every mammal, bird, reptile, and fish—and then some—can be found here.

The National Geographic Society's *Wild Animals of North America* (Washington DC: 1979) is another fascinating big book, with Geographic-quality color plates and graphics. A comfortable and beautifully illustrated book is *The Backyard Bestiary* by Ton de Joode and Anthonie Stolk (New York: Alfred A. Knopf, 1982). Kees de Kifte's watercolors are intimate glimpses into animal life.

More portable are Richard Headstrom's *Suburban Wildlife* (Englewood Cliffs, NJ: Prentice-Hall, Inc., 1984), a paperback guide to backyard creatures; *The Wildlife Observer's Guidebook* by Charles E. Roth (Englewood Cliffs, NJ: Prentice-Hall, Inc., 1982); and the take-along field guide, *The Audubon Society Field Guide to North American Mammals* (New York: Alfred A. Knopf, 1980). Clear photos, a protective plastic cover, and notes on breeding, habitat, and range make this a useful guide.

BIRDS. Most of us enjoy watching birds; we invariably begin to ask ourselves questions about their lives and identities. These books give us some of the answers: the indispensably classic *A Field Guide to the Birds* by Roger Tory Peterson (Boston: Houghton Mifflin Co., 1980), which includes field marks, maps, and verbal voice descriptions; *The Audubon Society Field Guide to North American Birds* by John Bull and John Farrand, Jr. (New York: Alfred A. Knopf, 1977); and the Golden Guides' *Families of Birds* by Oliver L. Austin (New York: Golden Press, 1971).

Volumes I and II of the *Guides to Bird Behavior* by Donald W. Stokes (Boston: Little, Brown, & Company, 1979 and 1983, paperback) are full of in-depth observations.

If you want to know about *housing* birds, *The Birdhouse Book* by Don McNeil (Seattle, Wash.: Pacific Search Press, 1979) is a good place to start; or check with your state's conservation commission. You might want to send for a copy of Conservation Bulletin #14 from the U. S. Department of the Interior, Fish and Wildlife Service: *Homes for Birds*.

A Complete Guide to Bird Feeding by John V. Dennis (New York: Alfred A. Knopf, 1975) really is complete.

SPIDERS AND INSECTS. For these, my favorite books are the Stokes Nature Guide series' *Guide to Observing Insect Lives* by Donald W. Stokes (Boston: Little, Brown & Company, 1983), which explains relationships and life cycles; *The Audubon Society Field Guide to North American Insects and Spiders* by Louis and Margery Milne (New York: Alfred A. Knopf, 1980), which is easy to use, with good, clear photos and complete notes; and three of the useful little paperbacks from the Golden Guides (New York: Golden Press) series: *Insects* (1956) by Herbert A. Zim and Clarence Cotton, *Butterflies and Moths* (1977) by Robert T. Mitchell and Zim, and *Spiders and Their Kin* (1968) by Herbert W. Levi and Lorna R. Levi.

Simon and Schuster's Guide to Insects by Ross H. Arnett, Jr. and Richard L. Jacques (New York: 1981) is a beautiful and useful paperback, but it may be difficult to find what you are looking for in the index if you don't know proper scientific names.

PLANTS

If the plant world captures your interest, you may find these books useful: *A Guide to Wildflowers and Weeds* by Booth Courtenay and James Zimmerman (New York: Van Nostrand Reinhold, 1972), which is one of the best I've found for identification (plants are listed by family and have excellent color photos). A very useful field guide for identification—and inspiration—is Jan Emberton's book, *Pods: Wildflowers and Weeds in Their Final Beauty* (New York: Charles Scribner's Sons, 1979). The plants are photographed in their flowering stages in the field, as a large, dried pod/seed head/stalk, and in a mixed arrangement. The inexpensive small guide from the Golden Guides series, *Weeds* by Alexander C. Martin, includes wonderful illustrations of plants, flowers, berries, or seeds and maps of the growing area.

The Peterson series book *A Field Guide to the Wildflowers* (Boston: Houghton-Mifflin, 1968) is still the bible: Showier flowers are in color; less common (and white) flowers are in black-and-white line drawings. I usually take along to the field the Peterson guide and the *Audubon Society Field Guide to North American Wildflowers* by William A. Niering and Nancy C. Olmstead (New York: Alfred A. Knopf, 1979).

A very good and easy-to-understand book on botany for the amateur naturalist is *The Plant Observer's Guidebook* by Charles E. Roth (Englewood Cliffs, NJ: Prentice-Hall, Inc., 1984). This one helps you understand the *why* as well as the *what*.

Another must-have book is *Suburban Wildflowers* by Richard Headstrom (Englewood Cliffs, N.J.: Prentice-Hall, Inc., 1984). The illustrations by Bobbi Angell of the New York Botanical Garden are superb.

Simon and Schuster's Guide to Trees (New York: 1978) has good color photos supplemented by line drawings. *Trees of North America,* one of the larger Golden Field Guide series (New York: Golden Press, 1968) is indispensable.

My favorite tree book is *A Photographic Guide to More Than 500 Trees of North America and Europe* by Roger Phillips (New York: Random House, 1978). This paperback is too big for a field guide, but it is excellent.

If nonflowering plants interest you, look at *Simon and Schuster's Guide to Mushrooms* by Giovanni Pacioni (U. S. editor, Gary Lincoff, New York, 1981). Excellent photos; information on habitat, season, and edibility—if I could have only one mushroom book, this would be it.

The Savory Wild Mushroom by Margaret McKenny (Seattle, Wash: University of Washington Press, 1971) is a paperback "oldie but goodie." Your library should be able to find it for you.

Still in print is *Mushroom Pocket Field Guide* by Howard E. Bigelow (New York: Macmillan, 1979, paper).

An inexpensive and comprehensive little guide is the Golden Guide entry on *Non-Flowering Plants* (New York: Golden Press, 1967). This small paperback is perennially available, and it includes algae, fungi, lichens, mosses, ferns, and more. *Forests of Lilliput: The Realm of Mosses and Lichens* by John Bland (Englewood Cliffs, NJ: Prentice-Hall, Inc., 1971) is an older, hardbound book your library will be able to find for you; it's well worth the search.

KEEPING A FIELD JOURNAL

For those interested in keeping their own field journals (a practice I can't recommend too highly), a must-have book is Clare Walker Leslie's *The Art of Field Sketching* (Englewood Cliffs, NJ: Prentice-Hall, 1984). Covering a wider and more art-related field is the same author's first book, *Nature Drawing, A Tool for Learning,* (also from Prentice-Hall, 1980). Both are available in paperback.

If you need to kick-start your drawing skills, try *Drawing on The Right Side of the Brain* by Betty Edwards (Los Angeles: J. P. Tarcher, 1979). This handy and inspiring paperback is still in print and should be easily available.

If you're looking for inspiration, see: *C. F. Tunicliffe Sketches of Bird Life* (New York: Watson-Guptill, 1981); Rein Poortvliet's *The Living Forest* (London: New English Library, 1979); Janet Marsh's *Nature Diary* (New York: William Morrow and Company, 1979); or *One Man's Island; A Naturalist's Year* by Keith Brockie (New York: Harper and Row, 1984).

RESOURCES

Many groups and organizations are available to help in your study of nature. Check with your local parks and recreation department; there may be a well-marked nature trail or an interpretive center nearby. County and state parks departments will be able to tell you more about what is available to you locally. There may be a privately owned nature sanctuary nearby; check the Yellow Pages. Look in the Yellow Pages also for the telephone number of the nearest Audubon Society chapter; consider joining to receive the local newsletter as well as the beautiful *Audubon* magazine. Your state conservation commission might have a free magazine for interested taxpayers, too.

Your local museum might have natural history information for your locale; the Kansas City Museum of History and Science has a natural history building and a planetarium. Perhaps your local university or college has extension courses or a museum. College biology departments often allow access to displays and information to members of the public at large.

Don't overlook the zoo. Although many city zoos have only exotic animals from far away, many more are beginning to display indigenous animals in natural settings as well.

Large art museums may offer courses on nature in art; at the very least there should be many excellent paintings of natural subjects and a library with public access (sometimes by appointment only; be sure to check).

Don't forget your local public library. Mine has been endlessly helpful in research for this book; those books not available locally have been provided through interlibrary loans.

In addition, these organizations may help:

Defenders of Wildlife, 1244 Nineteenth Street, N. E., Washington, DC 20036

Ducks Unlimited, P. O. Box 66300, Chicago, IL 60666

Earthwatch (Research Expeditions), Box 127, Belmont, MA 02178

National Audubon Society, 950 Third Avenue, New York, NY 10022

National Wildlife Federation, 1412 Sixteenth Street N. W., Washington, DC 20036

Sierra Club, Chapter Services, 530 Bush Street, San Francisco, CA 94108

Many of the natural history or outdoor interest magazines might be able to help you as well; subscribe, check your local library for copies, or even write the editor with questions. I've found most unfailingly helpful.

There are a number of wild flower seed suppliers.

Clyde Robin Seed Co., Inc. Box 2855, Castro Valley, CA 94546

Horizon Seeds, Inc., 1600 Cornhusker Highway, P. O. Box 81823, Lincoln, NE 68501

Midwest Wildflowers, Box 64m, Rockton, IL 61072

Wildlife Nurseries, P.O. Box 2724, Oshkosh, WI 54903

For plants, try:

Woodlanders, Inc., 1128 Colleton Ave., Aiken, SC 29801

Index